THE LIE *is* LOUD

Silence the Noise
Step into Who You Are

MONICA CONNOLLY

Published by She Rises Studios Publishing **www.SheRisesStudios.com**.

ISBN: 978-1-971349-20-6

Table of Contents

Foreword

Every once in a while, you meet someone and immediately know it's not a coincidence—it's alignment. That's how it was with Monica Connolly. From the very first moment, I could tell she carried both fire and depth—an unmistakable light that comes from walking through the dark and deciding to rise anyway.

Our first meeting happened in early 2024, and even then, I could sense she was standing on the edge of transformation. Within months, I watched her not only reclaim her health and confidence but also begin stepping boldly into her purpose. By the time she joined my Unstoppable Mastermind, I knew this woman was not just transforming—she was becoming a leader who would change lives.

Since that time, I've seen Monica soar. She's lost over 150 pounds, healed her body and mind, and built a business that blends science, soul, and purpose. She's a sought-after speaker, a podcast host, and a powerful coach guiding others from burnout to breakthrough. What impresses me most isn't just her success—it's the way she leads with integrity, empathy, and boldness. She shows up for her clients and community with the same heart she brings to every conversation: authentic, faith-rooted, and unstoppable.

Monica doesn't just talk about transformation; she *embodies* it. She's turned her pain into purpose, her healing into a mission, and her story into a movement. Her coaching work, her RESET and THRIVE frameworks, and her upcoming book all carry the same heartbeat: truth, freedom, and faith. She reminds us that healing isn't about perfection—it's about permission to start again.

The Lie Is Loud isn't just a book—it's a declaration. It's for every person who's ever believed they weren't enough. Monica's writing is raw and real, but also radiant with hope. She doesn't offer quick fixes; she offers transformation born from lived experience. Her words invite you to quiet the noise, rediscover your worth, and rise with purpose.

What I admire most about Monica is her obedience to her calling. She could have stayed silent, but instead she said yes—to healing, to growth, and to impact. She now mentors others to do the same, creating a ripple effect that reaches far beyond her coaching clients.

And I can tell you this with certainty: She's just getting started.

I see Monica stepping onto even bigger stages, leading global conversations on healing, identity, and resilience. I see her books reaching millions, her programs expanding internationally, and her story becoming a blueprint for others ready to rise from their own ashes. She's not building a brand—she's building a legacy.

To Monica: Thank you for leading with courage, faith, and authenticity. You are proof that when we align our purpose with our heart, there are no limits to how high we can rise.

And to you, the reader: As you turn these pages, prepare to be moved. Monica's story will remind you that the lie may be loud, but the truth—your truth—is louder.

With love and belief,
Amberly Lago

The Lie Is Loud

There is a moment most women can name, even if they have never spoken it out loud.

It is the moment you realize you have been living someone else's expectations.
The moment your body feels tired in a way rest does not fix.
The moment your inner voice feels critical, relentless, and familiar.
The moment you look in the mirror and quietly wonder, *When did I stop recognizing myself?*

That moment is not weakness.
It is awareness.

And it is where this book begins.

We live in a world that rewards noise. Louder opinions. Faster answers. Endless productivity. Constant comparison. From the time we are young, we are taught who to be, how to behave, what success should look like, and how much of ourselves we must sacrifice to be accepted, loved, or seen as worthy.

Over time, that noise becomes internal.
It sounds like self doubt.
It sounds like criticism.
It sounds like pressure to keep going even when your body and spirit are begging for rest.

That noise is not truth.
It is the lie.

The lie tells you that you are behind.
That you are too much or not enough.

That healing can wait.
That your needs are optional.
That who you are becoming should look like everyone else.

The truth is quieter.
But it is steady.
And it has been waiting for you.

* * *

I did not come to this work through theory or perfection. I came to it through lived experience.

For years, I was the strong one. The dependable one. The woman who kept going no matter what. I learned how to survive, how to show up, how to hold it together. On the outside, I looked capable and accomplished. On the inside, I was exhausted, disconnected, and slowly losing myself.

My body carried what my voice could not say. Chronic stress. Inflammation. Weight struggles. Emotional numbness. I was doing all the right things, yet nothing felt aligned. Healing did not begin when I tried harder. It began when I listened.

What I discovered changed everything.

The body remembers what the mind tries to outrun.
The nervous system cannot heal in chaos.
And transformation does not begin with doing more. It begins with becoming honest.

I learned that the loudest voices shaping our lives are often not our own. They come from expectations, trauma, comparison, faith misunderstandings, and years of conditioning that taught us to silence ourselves for the sake of survival.

This book is not about fixing you.
 You are not broken.

This book is about helping you **remember who you are** beneath the noise.

* * *

In *The Lie Is Loud*, you will not find quick fixes or performative positivity. You will find grounded truth, practical reflection, and compassionate challenge. You will be invited to slow down, reconnect with your body, and begin making choices from clarity instead of chaos.

You will learn how to:

- Recognize the lies that keep you stuck in survival mode
- Understand the role your nervous system plays in your patterns, habits, and health
- Rebuild trust with yourself through small, intentional shifts
- Release identities that no longer fit who you are becoming
- Step forward with confidence that is steady, not loud

This is not about becoming someone new.
It is about returning to yourself.

* * *

Each chapter builds intentionally, guiding you from awareness to integration. You will be asked to reflect, not rush. To listen, not perform. To choose presence over perfection.

Some pages may feel comforting.
Others may feel confronting.
Both are necessary.

As you read, I invite you to resist the urge to consume this book quickly. Let it meet you where you are. Pause when something resonates. Notice what your body responds to. Pay attention to the places you feel resistance. Those are often doorways to healing.

You do not need to have everything figured out to begin. You only need willingness.

* * *

If you are holding this book, chances are you already feel the quiet nudge that something more is possible. Not more doing. More alignment. More truth. More peace.

The lie may be loud.
But your truth is steady.

And if you are ready to listen, this book will help you hear it again.

Welcome.

The Fire That Forged Me

What is the hardest thing you've ever overcome? What did it teach you?

When was the last time you felt truly alive? What were you doing?

What is one belief about yourself that has held you back? How would your life change if you let it go?

My Declaration:

I've lived a long time agreeing with a lie that says I'm not enough.
Today, I choose to believe something different.
I was never created to prove my worth — I already have it.
The noise may still surround me, but I will start listening to Your whisper.
Because the lie is loud — *but Your truth is louder.*

You already know how to check the boxes.
You know how to smile when your soul is aching.
You know how to get things done, to hold it together, to be everything to everyone — *except yourself.*

You've read the devotionals. Listened to the podcasts. Bought the journals. Watched the reels.
But deep down, you're still asking:
Is this it? Is this all I was made for?

Let me tell you the truth that changed everything for me: *You were made for more* — not just more responsibility, but more life. More purpose. More joy. More fire.

And no, it's not too late. You're not too far gone. And you're not making it up.

I know the weight you carry, because I carried it too.

From the outside, I was doing everything "right."
On the inside, I was dying — *literally.*

My body was failing. I weighed over 325 pounds. I couldn't sleep more than a few hours at night.
I was binge eating to numb emotions I didn't have the tools or space to process.
I was staying busy, because if I slowed down, I'd have to feel what I'd been running from.

Then one day, I saw Jeremiah 29:11 on a plaque in a friend's office:

"For I know the plans I have for you," declares the Lord...

I had read that verse a thousand times before. But that day, it felt different.
Not a quote. *A catalyst.* A spark in a soul that had forgotten how to hope.

I hadn't healed yet. I hadn't lost weight. I hadn't fixed my habits.
But something about that moment made me sit up a little straighter.
Like maybe... *just maybe...* I wasn't beyond redemption.

I started showing up for myself in small ways.
It would take two more years before I walked into a room and finally felt seen and heard.
But that moment — that verse — whispered to me:
You're not done yet.

This book isn't about my coaching program (though I have one).
It's not about giving you my blueprint (though I've built one that

works).

It's not about fixing you.

This book is about calling you back to the truth.

You're not broken. *You're buried.*
And it's time to uncover the woman you were always meant to be.

I wrote this book for the woman who's silently unraveling beneath a perfectly composed life.
The one who's spent years being "the strong one."
The one who still believes in God — but hasn't felt Him in a while.
The one who's praying, *"If there's more for me... please show me."*

If that's you, I want you to know: That prayer? *I've prayed it too.*
And this book is part of the answer.

You don't need a formula. You need *truth*. You need *permission*.
You need proof that you're not alone, and that it's not too late.

Each chapter will confront a lie you've believed. We'll speak the truth. And I'll invite you to reflect, journal, and take one small, sacred step forward.

You don't have to be perfect. You just have to be *present*.

You've listened to the lies long enough. Let's turn the volume down on everything that's been keeping you stuck — and *turn the truth all the way up.*

Let's begin.

CHAPTER ONE

The Lie is Loud (Part One)

Lie: If you hear it often enough, it must be true.
Truth: The volume of a lie doesn't make it real.

The Rhythm of Each Chapter

Every chapter in this book follows a rhythm: declaration → story → teaching → practices and reflections → journal prompts. In this book, we begin with *my story of survival, performance, and the body that carried both trauma and silence.* Then, I'll offer teaching and practices that help you recognize the lies you've believed about your worth, and the truth that can set you free.

Declaration

God, I've lived a long time agreeing with a lie that says I'm not enough. Today, I choose to believe something different.

I was never created to prove my worth—I already have it.
The noise may still surround me, but I will start listening to Your whisper.
Because the lie is loud—but Your truth is louder.

Amen.

* * *

I shouldn't be here.
By all accounts, I should have been taken out long ago.

There were moments when I stood on the edge, when my body, my mind, and my spirit felt like they had nothing left. I've faced chronic illness, unrelenting pressure, and loss that shattered me. I've carried more than I *thought possible* and stayed standing anyway.

And yet, here I am.
Not just surviving—but rising.

I now know I was made for more.
And so are you.

This book isn't just about my story. It's about yours. It's about the fire you've walked through, the weight you've carried, and the voice inside you whispering, *There has to be more than this.*

That whisper isn't wishful thinking. It's truth trying to break through.

There were so many moments that could've been my end.
The quiet mornings when I wondered if I could keep going.
The nights I cried in silence, overwhelmed by the weight of what I carried.
The countless days I wore a smile and answered, *"I'm fine,"* when I was anything but.

At first, I thought it was just stubbornness that kept me alive. Then I thought maybe it was luck.
But eventually, I realized: *I'm still here because the story isn't finished.*

And neither is yours.

Survival Wore the Mask of Strength

On the outside, my life looked like strength. I was independent, driven, and always the one who could keep going. People called me *"strong,"* and I believed them. I wore that word like armor.

But that strength wasn't a choice—it was *survival.*

As a kid, I learned quickly: You can't always count on safety, love has a price, and control is the only protection. That turned into a lie I carried for years, that what I did for people was what made me worthy.

So I built a mask. I became the girl who smiled even when she was hurting, who got good grades, who did what was expected, who stayed quiet when her heart was screaming.

By high school, that mask came with me everywhere. At work, I was the dependable one. In friendships, the listener. At home, the steady one who held it all together. People admired me for it. They called me selfless, dependable, resilient. Every time someone praised me for being *"so strong,"* I felt a flicker of validation.

But here's the truth: I wasn't strong. I was *surviving.* And there's a difference.

The lie was loud: If you keep giving, achieving, and smiling, you'll finally be enough.
But I've learned: The louder the lie, the more silent the truth becomes.

The Lie Takes Root

The lie didn't show up all at once. It arrived slowly—drip by drip—through repetition, comparison, and subtle rejection.

By middle school, I already believed I wasn't smart enough.
Not good enough.
Not athletic enough.
Too big. Too loud.
And somehow, still... never enough.

In elementary school, my test scores measured that of a college level. On paper, I was advanced. But no matter how high I scored, it was never enough. I still wasn't *"smart enough."*

The bar kept moving. I kept shrinking.

There were voices—familiar ones—that made sure the lie stayed loud. Whispers. Comparisons. Comments not meant to be cruel, but they left marks anyway. No reward for effort—only reminders I could do better, be better, weigh less, act more like someone else.

Eventually, I stopped trying.

I floated through school. Did the homework but didn't turn it in. I stopped showing up for my own potential because I believed it didn't matter.

Once, I poured myself into a school project I was proud of. My teacher accused me of plagiarism, insisting there was no way I could have produced work of that quality.

That moment stuck. Not because it was dramatic, but because it validated the lie I already believed: *You don't belong. You don't measure up. No one will ever believe you.*

So I became what I thought the world wanted: the high-functioning, strong one.
The helper. The doer. The achiever. The one who could hold it all together.
All while *silently unraveling.*

Numbing Out

There are entire chapters of my life I can't remember.

I now know that dissociation protected me. My mind created distance from trauma by numbing it out. Even now, my children mention memories I have no access to. Holidays, birthdays, special trips. I know I was there, but I wasn't present. There are pictures, and that's the only proof I have.

I took pictures obsessively. It wasn't just about preserving memories, it was about documenting evidence. Because I couldn't trust my body to feel joy or recall peace. I captured moments to make sure I wouldn't lose them.

But I rarely allowed myself to be in the photos. I hid behind the lens. I avoided the camera because I couldn't bear to see myself. The woman in those photos didn't match the one I longed to be. *She looked tired, ashamed, heavy—not just physically, but spiritually.*

So I kept myself out of the frame.
Literally.
And emotionally.

I became the historian of everyone else's life while slowly disappearing from my own.

The Performance of Perfection

For eight years, I owned and operated a licensed daycare and preschool. On the surface, it looked like I had it all together—spotless home, themed snacks, handmade crafts, and holiday gift bags for every child.

I was meticulous about appearances—my children's, my husband's, and mine. Clothes were always perfectly pressed and laundered. People assumed I thrived on being busy.

I didn't. I just didn't know how to stop.

Perfection became my camouflage. If I kept everything looking okay on the outside, no one would ask about the inside. And for the most part, they didn't.

Behind the scenes, I was drowning in exhaustion. I opened my doors before dawn, cared for toddlers all day, and closed after dark. Parents saw a smiling, organized teacher with lesson plans, crafts, and creative snacks. What they didn't see was the woman who collapsed on the couch after cleaning up, too tired to eat dinner herself.

I told myself I was doing it for the families, for the kids, for my own children who deserved the best. But underneath the service, there was fear: *If I stopped performing, I'd be exposed.*

That mask of competence followed me everywhere.

Later, when I worked in the emergency room, the mask came with me. I wore perfectly pressed professional clothing, hair done, makeup on— the picture of competence. I greeted patients with calm confidence, charted with efficiency, and kept pace with the endless stream of emergencies.

To everyone else, I looked like a woman who thrived under pressure. But behind that image was a body that betrayed me daily.

The migraines that came like lightning strikes. The joint pain that flared without warning. The fatigue that no amount of caffeine could shake.

I learned to ignore it, to silence it, to tuck it behind a polished smile.

People saw a professional who "had it together." They didn't see the woman driving home at dawn with the steering wheel digging into her palms, fighting to keep her eyes open through exhaustion. They didn't see the way my hands shook when I finally crawled into bed. They didn't see the pills on my nightstand or the heating pad tucked under the sheets.

I believed the lie that if I just kept moving, if I just kept producing, no one would notice I was unraveling.
And most of the time, they didn't.

Food as Comfort, Food as Control

There were nights when I would send my daughter to the store just to get me chocolate bars. Always after dinner, always with the same urgency.

When I was anxious, I wanted salty foods.
When I was angry, I craved heavy, greasy food.
When I felt unloved or unseen, I reached for sweet treats.

It wasn't hunger—it was coping.

Food became my drug of choice. It never judged me. It never abandoned me. It didn't ask questions or raise an eyebrow.

It was there when I needed to fill the silence or numb the ache.

I told myself it was comfort. I told myself it was a treat after a long day. But it wasn't about the food at all. *It was about the need to escape my own body, my own thoughts, my own life.*

Food gave me something I could control in a world where everything else felt uncontrollable.

But eventually, my body gave out.

The Bottom Step

After a trip to Disney World for my daughter's second birthday, I came home and couldn't walk up the stairs.

I remember standing at the bottom, one hand on the railing, one foot lifted—and my leg refused to cooperate. My knees throbbed. My joints screamed. My whole body felt like it was shutting down.

I sat on the bottom step and cried not from sadness, not even from anger, but from pure defeat.

I was 20-something years old and couldn't climb a flight of stairs.
What kind of mother can't carry her child upstairs?
What kind of woman falls apart before her life has even really begun?

I had suffered "growing pains" my whole life, but they never stopped. As I entered adulthood, those random aches grew into full-body exhaustion. The pain was constant. The fatigue was soul-deep.

Doctors told me it was stress, that I needed to lose weight, that maybe I was just "run down." But I knew something was wrong.

Eventually, one doctor finally admitted it and referred me to a specialist four hours away. That's where I was diagnosed with fibromyalgia—a word I had never heard before.

The explanation was vague. It was "likely trauma-related." There wasn't much research. Not many answers. Just a label.

And so I did what I had always done.
I pushed through.

The Body Remembers

In 2020, while taking my son to a geneticist to explore his chronic pain and fatigue, I finally received another diagnosis: Ehlers-Danlos Syndrome.

Suddenly, the puzzle pieces fit. The frequent joint dislocations. The unexplained injuries. The constant exhaustion. *The way my body seemed to respond to life as if it were trauma—because for me, it often was.*

EDS wasn't just a diagnosis. It was an answer to decades of pain I had been told to ignore.

But answers didn't equal relief.

Stress and trauma didn't just make things worse—they *rewired me.* Both fibro and EDS were intensified by the very things I was swimming in every single day: caretaking, suppression, perfectionism, grief.

The flare-ups were unpredictable. Some days, I did everything "right"—ate clean, moved gently, rested—and still couldn't get out of bed. Other days, I pushed past the pain, only to collapse the next.

My body kept screaming, but I kept silencing it.

The Doctor's Warning

I stopped making appointments. I told myself I was too busy, too needed by everyone else. But the truth was deeper: *I didn't believe I was worth the time.*

Until one day, a doctor looked me straight in the eye and said:

"If you don't make changes, you're going to die."

No empathy. No pause. Just blunt truth.

There was no dramatic reaction. No meltdown. No collapse.

I went home and folded a load of laundry.

Because that's what I did. I processed survival through movement, through productivity, through staying numb.

I never told anyone. Not my husband. Not even the people closest to me.

I buried it with everything else.

Cracks in the Armor

There's only so long you can carry silence before the cracks start to show.

I remember crying once, years earlier, in a hospital bathroom. My sister and nephew had been in a devastating car accident. We thought we might lose them both.

I broke down in that bathroom—heaving sobs, shaking hands, the kind of grief you can't plan for. But that was the only time I allowed myself to fall apart.

And even then—it wasn't for me.

I never cried for myself.
Never mourned the life I thought I'd have.
Never allowed space to feel the disappointment of being so tired, so early, so often.

Because I didn't think it would change anything.
And because I didn't think it was allowed.

Victims wait to be rescued. I didn't believe I had that option.

So I just kept moving.

I eventually left night shifts behind, but I stayed in corporate and administrative healthcare—still performing, still holding everything together, even as my body kept breaking.

I was a full-time student, while my own kids were in school, so I kept attending school meetings, paying bills, and showing up for people who had no idea I was fading inside. I kept putting on mascara and a strong smile even when it felt like I was breaking.

The Turn

This wasn't healing—not yet. That would come years later.

What kept me here in those dark moments wasn't a breakthrough or a miracle. *It was my kids.*

The only thing stronger than the urge to give up was the knowledge that they needed me here—no matter what version of me showed up.

So I stayed.
Broken. Exhausted. Numb.
But here.

Sometimes people talk about resilience as if it's shiny and admirable. *My resilience didn't look like that.* It looked like crawling out of bed because two little people were counting on me to feed them breakfast. It looked like dragging my body through a workday even when my joints begged me to stop. It looked like putting on lipstick so no one would ask questions I didn't have the energy to answer.

My kids didn't need a perfect mother. They just needed me alive. And that was enough reason to keep going when everything else told me to quit.

Something sacred happens when a woman stops performing strength and starts embodying truth.

Truth doesn't shout. It whispers. And when you finally get still enough to listen—you hear it.

It sounds like freedom. Like peace. Like permission.

This was the moment I began walking toward myself.

Not the version who hustled for approval.
Not the one who only felt worthy when she was exhausted.
Not the one who believed healing was for everyone else.

But the version I was created to become.

The one who was made for more—not because she had to prove it, but because she was always worthy of it.

Teaching: Survival Looks Like Strength

Survival often masquerades as strength. We applaud people for being independent, capable, and tireless.
But many of us learned those habits out of necessity, not choice.

Trauma taught us to hold it all together because falling apart didn't feel safe.
Over time, we confused survival with identity.
We forgot that we are more than what we can produce or protect.

You don't have to earn your worth by being everything for everyone.
You are not what you manage.
You are not what you hide.
You are not the mask.

You are the person underneath it—whole, loved, and still here for a reason.

Teaching: When Survival Becomes an Identity

Survival is not the same thing as strength.

Survival is what the body and nervous system do when safety is uncertain. It is adaptive. Intelligent. Necessary. But it was never meant to become who you are.

Many women reading this learned early that rest was dangerous, needs were inconvenient, and slowing down meant falling apart. So survival became the strategy. And eventually, it became the identity.

You didn't choose this consciously.
Your body chose it for you.

But here's the truth that changes everything:

What keeps you alive is not what will set you free.

Strength rooted in survival is rigid.
Strength rooted in truth is steady.

Survival says, "I can't stop."
Truth says, "I don't have to prove my worth."

This is where healing begins. Not by dismantling your resilience, but by releasing the belief that exhaustion is the price of belonging.

Clarity begins when you recognize that the version of you who survived was never the final version. She was the bridge.

You are allowed to outgrow the patterns that once protected you.
You are allowed to become someone who no longer needs armor.
You are allowed to live without constantly earning your place.

This book will not ask you to relive your pain.
It will ask you to tell the truth about it.

And the first truth is this:

You were never weak.
You were surviving.

And now, you get to choose something more.

Practices and Reflections

Mirror Check:
Stand in front of a mirror. Instead of asking, "How do I look?" ask, *"How do I feel?"*
Write down what comes up without judgment. Let honesty—not performance—speak first.

Pause Practice:
Set a timer for five minutes. Sit in silence with your hands open on your lap.
Notice how hard or easy it feels to simply *be,* without doing.
If stillness feels uncomfortable, that's okay. That's information, not failure.

Compassion Phrase:
Each morning, place your hand on your chest and repeat:
"I am valuable because of who I am, not what I do."
Say it out loud. Say it until the words start to sound familiar.
You are retraining your brain to believe the truth.

Reflection Questions:

- Where did you first learn that your worth depended on performance?
- What situations still trigger you to hide your true self?
- What would it feel like to believe you are loved simply because you exist?

Journal Prompts

1. When did the lie first take root for you?

    ____

    ____

2. What are the moments, voices, or patterns that made it feel
    believable?

    ____

    ____

3. What would it look like to stop agreeing with it—*starting today?*

    ____

    ____

Take your time. Don't rush to the answer. The goal isn't perfection—
it's awareness.

CHAPTER TWO

The Mirror Lies, Too

Lie: You are too far gone.
Truth: You are still becoming.

Declaration

I am not too far gone.
I am not defined by my diagnoses, my weight, or my reflection.
I am worthy of healing, compassion, and life.
The lie may be loud, but the truth is louder.

* * *

The lie was loudest in the doctor's office.

I had already been through gestational diabetes twice, so when my physician looked at me with clinical certainty and told me it was now type 2 diabetes, I couldn't say I was shocked. But knowing it was likely didn't soften the blow. I sat there, nodding as if I were calm, while inside it felt like a gavel had come down: guilty.

Because of my medical background, I knew exactly what the lab results meant. I understood the A1C number, the risk factors, and the potential complications that could follow me like a shadow. I had counseled patients about the very diagnosis I was now receiving. But this time, it wasn't a chart in my hands. It was my own body on trial.

And knowledge cuts both ways. It prepared me, yes, but it also condemned me. I could hear the voice in my head growing louder than the doctor's: *You knew better. You should have prevented this. How could you let it get this far?*

I smiled politely, thanked him for his time, tucked the paperwork into my bag, and walked out of the office like I had everything under control. But the drive home was a blur. My hands gripped the wheel tightly, and my mind replayed every "what if" from the past decade. What if I had made different choices? What if I had prioritized myself sooner? What if my worth wasn't tangled up in holding everyone else together?

The thing about diabetes is that it doesn't show up suddenly—it builds. And I knew that. But knowing it didn't stop the shame.

When fibromyalgia and Ehlers-Danlos Syndrome joined the list, my reaction surprised me. Instead of despair, I felt relief. For years, I had been carrying pain I couldn't explain—burning muscles, crushing fatigue, migraines that blurred my vision, joints slipping as if my body were constantly betraying me. For so long, I had wondered if it was in my head. Now, finally, there were names.

Fibro. EDS.

Names gave me something to research. Names gave me permission to learn. Names gave me proof. But they also gave me labels I carried in silence.

Fibromyalgia explained the mornings I woke with muscles screaming as if I had run marathons in my sleep. The kind of bone-deep ache that no medication, no nap, no "quick fix" could touch. It explained the fatigue that pulled me under, no matter how much I rested. The brain fog that left me grasping for words mid-sentence, wondering if I was losing myself piece by piece.

EDS explained the joints that slipped out of place, the constant injuries, the bruises I couldn't remember earning. It explained the way my body resisted stability, the way daily life sometimes felt like walking on glass.

Still, even with answers, the loudest label wasn't fibro, EDS, or diabetes. It was weight. It was the reflection I couldn't bear to see.

Every skipped photo.
Every event where I blended into the background.
Every time I layered clothes, not to express myself, but to disguise myself.

That was my scarlet letter. Not just the weight itself, but the story I attached to it—that I had failed, that I had lost control, that I had wasted my potential.

And yet, my body wasn't the only weight I carried.

* * *

Caregiving is invisible until you've lived it. People see resilience, but they don't see the hours. They don't see the stacks of paperwork, the insurance calls, the quiet desperation of piecing together a new normal you never asked for.

When my husband became ill, life split into before and after. Overnight, I stepped into roles that needed to be held. What I did not anticipate was how rarely responsibility would be reclaimed once the crisis passed. Our partnership shifted. His recovery became my responsibility to manage, layered on top of everything else.

At the same time, my children had medical needs of their own. Specialists, procedures, therapies. The scheduling alone could have been a full-time job. And in the middle of it all, I was still working. Still showing up for others. Still performing strength.

Underneath, grief was constant. I learned to carry it quietly, not because it was unspeakable, but because there was no consistent space where it could be met with responsibility or care. So I shoved it down. I buried it under competence, under to-do lists, under the mask of "I'm fine."

People called me strong, and I wore that word like armor. But what they didn't see was the cost. They didn't see me collapse into bed after a day of managing appointments, cooking dinner, helping with homework, and hiding pain that flared so badly I could barely climb the stairs. They didn't see the nights I lay awake, bargaining with God for the energy to do it all again tomorrow.

Strength without rest eventually cracks. And my cracks showed up everywhere—my weight, my exhaustion, my health, my spirit.

I remember one night vividly. I had put the kids to bed, finished the dishes, and sat down at the kitchen table with a stack of forms from yet another specialist. My hands trembled as I tried to fill them out, my joints aching, my brain fog so thick I read the same line three times without comprehension. And in that moment, the thought whispered: *What if I just disappeared? What if I stopped?*

But then, as quickly as it came, another thought overpowered it: My kids need me. No matter the version of me they get, they still need me here.

That's what kept me alive when the lie told me otherwise. Not self-belief. Not motivation. Just the stubborn love of a mother who refused to leave her children without her.

I stayed for them long before I ever learned to stay for myself.

* * *

This was the season when food became both my comfort and my punishment. When the house was quiet, when the paperwork was stacked, when the grief was heaviest, I turned to food. It was there when nothing else was. It never left. It numbed.

I can still recall the cycle: walking into the kitchen, grabbing whatever was closest—cookies, chips, leftovers. Eating fast, as if I could outrun the feelings rising in my chest. For a moment, it worked. The taste dulled the ache. But afterward came the shame. The regret. The vow to do better. And then, the next wave of stress would hit, and I'd find myself in the same spot again.

It wasn't about hunger. It was about trying to silence a body that felt like too much.

And every bite reinforced the lie that I was too far gone.

* * *

What I couldn't see then was that none of it was wasted. Not the diagnoses, not the exhaustion, not even the shame. Every single piece of my story—the caregiving, the chronic pain, the food battles, the grief—was shaping me for the work I now do. I hadn't missed my potential. I was being prepared for it.

But in that season, all I could hear was the lie.

Teaching: Momentum Over Motivation

Motivation fades. Healing rarely begins in fireworks. It begins in momentum—small choices stacked on top of one another until they carry you forward.

- Every time you face the mirror and choose compassion, you build momentum.
- Every time you whisper truth instead of agreeing with the lie, you build momentum.
- Every time you choose to stay present in your life, you build momentum.

Momentum matters more than motivation because once it starts rolling, it carries you further than you thought you could go. Healing is not instant; it is practiced.

Practices and Reflections

Mirror Work: Stand before a mirror. Look into your eyes and say one truth aloud: *"I am not too far gone."* Notice the resistance and repeat it daily.

Tiny Shifts: Choose one 1% action that honors your body today—drinking water, resting for 10 minutes, or going for a short walk. Write it down, then celebrate it as momentum.

Self-Compassion Break: When you catch yourself in shame, pause. Place your hand on your heart and repeat: *"This is hard. I am not alone. I am still becoming."*

Reflection Questions:

These are meant to be read slowly and answered briefly, even mentally at first.

They create awareness, not long processing.

- When did I first learn to stay quiet instead of speaking honestly?
- Who benefited from my silence?
- What did silence protect me from at the time?
- Where in my life do I still choose peace over truth?
- What does my body feel when I consider speaking fully and freely?
- What am I afraid would happen if I stopped minimizing myself?
- What feels truer right now: staying silent or being seen?

Finish this sentence honestly:
"If I trusted myself more, I would..."

Closing Integration Prompt (Optional but Powerful)

Write one sentence you can return to this week:
"I am allowed to be seen, heard, and honest—even when it feels uncomfortable."

No pressure to change anything yet.
Just notice what shifts when the truth is named.

Journal Prompts

These are for written processing and emotional honesty.

This is where depth happens.

1. Write about a moment when you knew the truth but chose silence anyway. What was at stake?

   ____

   ____

2. What words have I swallowed over the years? Let them come out uncensored here.

   ____

   ____

3. How has staying quiet shaped my identity, relationships, or sense of worth?

   ____

   ____

4. What parts of me learned that being "easy," "strong," or "low maintenance" was safer?

____

____

5. If my silence could speak, what would it say it was trying to protect?

____

____

6. What truth feels ready to be acknowledged, even if I am not ready to act on it yet?

____

____

<u>CHAPTER THREE</u>

The Body Remembers

Lie: My body is broken beyond repair.
Truth: My body remembers how to heal.

Declaration

I am not broken.
I am not beyond repair.
My body remembers how to heal.
I give myself permission to support healing—not just manage symptoms.

* * *

When we got back from Disney, I thought I had proven something to myself. I had pushed through exhaustion, swollen joints, and a body that begged for rest. I stood in the lines, walked the parks, smiled for the photos, and made it through the parades. On the outside, I looked like the determined mom who would not let pain ruin her children's memories.

But once we returned home, the facade cracked. I went to walk up the stairs in our house, and my body simply refused.

It wasn't willpower or laziness—it was like my legs had turned to cinderblocks. Each attempt to climb felt impossible. My muscles trembled, my joints screamed, and my lungs burned. The body that had carried me through Disney could no longer carry me up a single flight of stairs.

That was the moment I couldn't hide it anymore. My mask slipped. My body had finally screamed loudly enough that even I couldn't ignore it. And worse, my children saw it. They were used to the version of me that always kept moving, the mom who made things happen even if it meant collapsing in private later. But this time, there was no hiding. They saw me defeated on the stairs, unable to push through, and it broke something in me.

Up until then, I thought if I tried hard enough, if I stayed strong enough, I could outrun the pain. I thought sheer willpower could get me through anything. But this time, willpower wasn't enough.

Doctors finally began to take me seriously, but their answers came in the form of more prescriptions. Instead of asking *why* my body was breaking down, they set out to manage the collapse. I was referred to an arthritis specialist, and with that came an avalanche of medications: steroids to calm inflammation, NSAIDs to dull pain, muscle relaxers to force my body to unclench, and sleeping medications to make me rest.

Add those to the high-dose asthma medications and the multiple prescriptions I was already on for diabetes, and suddenly my days were ruled by bottles. My bathroom counter looked like a miniature pharmacy, rows of labels and childproof caps lined up like soldiers. Every morning and every evening, I swallowed handfuls of pills, hoping they would give me enough strength to make it through another day.

They didn't heal me; they managed me.

And management is not the same as healing.

Steroids gave me temporary relief, but they left me with side effects that only added to my misery—weight gain, mood swings, a face that puffed until I barely recognized myself. NSAIDs dulled some pain but tore up my stomach in the process. Muscle relaxers made me groggy and disconnected, my limbs heavy like sandbags. Sleeping medication forced my body to shut down, but it never gave me real rest; I woke up groggy, sometimes disoriented, wondering if I had slept at all.

And through all of this, I was still on multiple medications for asthma and diabetes, battling daily against the feeling that my body was slipping further and further out of my control.

Eventually, antidepressants were added as a last resort to help control pain. That was the prescription that stole something deeper from me. They didn't just dull the pain—they dulled *me*. My emotions flattened. My memory blurred. I was no longer just living with pain; I was living without joy.

I still worked. I still parented. I still smiled when I needed to. But behind closed doors, I was exhausted, frustrated, and hollowed out. My body was weighed down not only by illness but also by the endless cycle of bottles, refills, and side effects.

I think back now and realize how much shame lived in me during that season. Shame that my body couldn't perform the way I demanded. Shame that I needed so many medications to "function." Shame that even with all the pills, I still couldn't live the life I wanted. I wore that shame like another invisible illness, one that no doctor ever treated but that ate at me every day.

And no one ever suggested there might be another way. Not once.

No one mentioned gut health, inflammation, or the possibility that trauma could live in the body and manifest as pain. No one suggested natural or osteopathic treatments. The framework I was handed was pharmaceutical management, period. When one pill caused new issues, the answer was another pill to mask the side effects. And when that caused complications, another prescription was added.

The deeper truth was this: My pain wasn't random. My body wasn't broken by accident. It was carrying years of stress, grief, trauma, and depletion. But no one ever asked me about those things. And at the time, I didn't even know how to name them myself.

Survival had trained me to accept this as normal. Pills to wake up. Pills to get through the day. Pills to go to bed. Pills to handle the side effects of the other pills. It was a cycle I didn't even realize I was trapped in.

But deep down, there was still a whisper I couldn't silence. Something in me knew I wasn't meant to live this way forever. I didn't yet know the language of holistic health. I didn't understand root-cause healing or nervous system regulation. But I knew that what I was doing—layering pills on top of pills—wasn't life.

The first time I pushed back was when I decided to wean off the narcotics. Compared to what came later, it was a surprisingly manageable process. It wasn't easy, but it didn't make me feel like I was dying. Slowly, I decreased the dosage. Slowly, I discovered that the world didn't end when I faced pain without a pill. It was my first small victory, my first reminder that I wasn't completely powerless.

But then came the antidepressants.

At first, I thought it would be like the narcotics—a matter of tapering down, adjusting, and moving on. I had no idea how deeply antidepressants had entangled themselves with my nervous system. The withdrawal was grueling. Nausea, dizziness, and sickness followed me like shadows. Some days, I could barely function. It wasn't just discomfort; it was destabilization. It took nearly a year of slow, painstaking reduction before I was finally free of them.

That year nearly broke me. And yet, it also shaped me. Every day, I had to choose: Do I give in and go back to the dose, or do I push forward into freedom? Every week I made it through felt like a rebellion, a reminder that my body still belonged to me.

I leaned heavily on natural supplements that targeted inflammation and pain without the horrible side effects. They weren't a magic fix, but they gave me just enough support to keep going. I clung to the hope that there was something better than numbing my life away.

Looking back, I can see how significant those choices were. But at the time, it didn't feel heroic—it felt exhausting. Every day was a decision to keep pressing forward, even when my body wanted to collapse back into the numbness. Yet underneath the sickness, there was a flicker of something I hadn't felt in years: possibility.

The body remembers. Mine remembered the years of masking, numbing, and silencing. It remembered the grief and trauma I hadn't given myself permission to express. But it also remembered resilience. Each pill I let go of was a step toward reclaiming myself. Each day of withdrawal was a day of choosing not to give up.

I wouldn't have called it healing at that point. It didn't feel like healing. It felt like crawling through fire. But sometimes, that's what healing begins as a decision to keep walking through the flames until you find solid ground again.

And what I didn't know then was that this painful process was planting seeds that wouldn't fully bloom until years later. Seeds of awareness. Seeds of curiosity. Seeds that would eventually lead me to question everything I had been taught about health, healing, and what my body was truly capable of.

The first time I tried to imagine a life without antidepressants, I honestly couldn't. They had become as routine as brushing my teeth. Every morning, every night, my locked pill container came out of the cupboard, and I would line up the bottles. Seven or eight at a time, sometimes more when you counted the inhalers and the insulin shots. It was mechanical. I even had a written schedule taped inside the cupboard door because I wasn't just managing my medications. I was also keeping track of my husband's and my kids'. What began as support slowly became expectation, and expectation hardened into routine without conversation or accountability. It felt like my entire household revolved around medication schedules.

I never thought of it as shameful. That's the lie I had been sold—that it was normal. Normal to need a pill for every symptom. Normal to hand over your body to prescriptions and still wake up exhausted, bloated, foggy, and in pain. Normal to expect no real improvement, only management. For years, I accepted that story.

But when I began the process of weaning off the antidepressants, everything changed.

The withdrawal was brutal. Constant nausea made food feel like an enemy. The dizziness was so intense that I had no business driving, but I didn't have a choice. I was the only driver in the house, and life doesn't stop because your brain feels like it's spinning out of your skull. After work, I would collapse on the couch, unable to do anything but wait for bedtime. On weekends, I wanted so desperately to spend time with my kids, to be the mom who could play and laugh with them. Instead, I spent far too many hours lying on that same couch, fighting my body and losing.

Every single day, I debated going back on them. The temptation was real. The idea of giving in and numbing out again whispered to me every time the nausea peaked, every time I stumbled from the dizziness, every time my kids asked for me and I couldn't get up. But the thought that kept me going was this: I was tired of living like that. Tired of masking. Tired of being a shell. If I went back, I knew I would never get free.

It took almost a year to finally taper off fully. A year of feeling like I was crawling through glass. A year of asking myself whether freedom was worth the cost. And yet, little by little, my body adjusted. With the help of natural supplements that targeted inflammation, I was able to slowly replace what the antidepressants had stolen from me.

Looking back, I can see that was the turning point—not because it felt triumphant, but because it was the first time I began to understand that *healing* is not the same as *management.*

But I didn't come to that realization alone.

One afternoon, when I was at one of my lowest points, I listened to a voicemail from a woman I hadn't spoken to since high school. We hadn't stayed in touch, and she had no idea how sick I was, no idea that my life was held together by prescription bottles and sheer willpower. Yet there she was, saying she was trying something new and thought of me.

At first, I was skeptical. Of course, I was—who wouldn't be after everything I had tried? I couldn't afford to buy what she was suggesting outright, so I put the order on a credit card. I told myself I would use the 60-day money-back guarantee, because surely it wouldn't work. But desperation is a powerful motivator. I didn't realize then how much that one choice would change the course of my story.

As I began to learn more about holistic health and supplements, I realized how little I had been taught about actually healing my body. My doctor had told me that if I didn't change something, I would die. I carried that sentence like a death sentence. The problem was, no one could tell me what *something* to change. Everywhere I looked, there was conflicting advice—cut carbs, eat carbs, avoid fat, eat fat, work out harder, rest more. It was overwhelming.

That's when I realized I would have to take my health into my own hands.

I researched accredited schools, pored over the options, and finally enrolled in a holistic health and wellness certification program. I wasn't signing up because I wanted to coach anyone at that time. I signed up because I was desperate and determined to heal myself.

It felt like learning a foreign language. Root causes, functional medicine, mind-body connection—these were concepts that no doctor had ever explained to me. But I loved it. I felt like I was peeling back layers of truth that had been hidden from me my whole life. I thought about my favorite TV show, *House MD*. Dr. House always asked the questions no one else thought to ask. He dug into people's lives, searched for connections, challenged assumptions. For the first time, I realized I needed to be Dr. House for myself. I couldn't just accept what I had been told—I had to investigate my own body and my own history.

Even with this new education, though, I wasn't consistent. I dipped in and out of using supplements. I read the material, nodded along at the concepts, and still struggled to fully believe. It wasn't until 2023 that everything finally clicked into place.

The difference wasn't just supplements—it was coaching.

That year, I got in the room with women who were being coached, who were breaking molds, living out of the box, and chasing dreams I hadn't even allowed myself to consider. Being around them was like permission. Permission to think differently. Permission to believe that maybe I could live differently, too.

Within weeks, I hired a coach. And everything began to shift.

I had been carrying around beliefs that were never mine to begin with. Lies that had been spoken over me so many times that I mistook them for truth. Coaching showed me how to question those lies. How to hold them up to the light and ask, "Is this really mine? Is this really true?" Most of the time, the answer was no.

And then, almost immediately after I started coaching, my father passed away unexpectedly.

Before coaching, that kind of grief would have shut me down. I would have gone through the motions, dissociated, swallowed the pain, and let it fester in my body. But this time, I had tools. I was able to sit with my grief without letting it consume me. I processed my emotions instead of numbing them. I felt the waves of loss and allowed them to move through me instead of lodging in my body as more pain. Coaching didn't take away the grief, but it transformed how I carried it.

At the same time, my body was finally responding. As the trauma layers began to loosen, my body released 150 pounds in two years. For years, every New Year's resolution I made was to lose 100 pounds, and every year, I failed. Because I didn't have the tools. Because I didn't know my body was holding onto weight as a form of protection. Healing the trauma allowed my body to finally let go.

But the weight loss was more than numbers on a scale. It was identity. It was finding my voice again. It was rediscovering what I wanted, what I needed, what I valued. It was mobility—freedom I hadn't realized I had lost until I got it back. When I look at old photos now, I can't fathom how I carried that weight and still did things like camping or hiking. I don't know how I physically did it. But I did, because that's what survival demanded.

Now, survival has been replaced by something better: healing.

Every three months, I get labs done. And every time, the numbers get better. Doctors once told me I would need medication for the rest of my life. Now, I am down to just three prescriptions, instead of the handfuls I used to swallow every morning and night. And every improvement isn't just validation—It's hope. Proof that my body isn't broken. Proof that healing is possible when you stop chasing symptoms and start supporting the root.

Today, I don't see my journey as one of failure. I see it as preparation. Every diagnosis, every bottle of pills, every couch-bound weekend—it all built the foundation for the work I do now. I know what it feels like to lose yourself to illness and medication. I know what it feels like to claw your way back. And I know what it feels like to rise again.

Healing, I've learned, isn't about perfection. It's about remembering who you were created to be and giving your body, mind, and spirit permission to return to that design.

And that is the message I want every woman holding this book to hear: You are not broken beyond repair. Your body remembers how to heal. Your mind can be renewed. Your spirit can rise again.

Teaching: Management is Not Healing

Doctors often manage symptoms instead of asking deeper questions. But management is not the same as healing. Our bodies carry grief, trauma, and stress—and when we don't address the root, symptoms multiply. Healing begins when we stop silencing our body's signals and start listening. It's not about perfection, it's about creating space for restoration.

Practices and Reflections

Body Scan with Gratitude: Lie down and slowly scan your body from head to toe. At each point of tension or pain, place your hand there and thank your body for carrying you this far.

Release and Replace: Write down one thing you've been "managing" (pain, fatigue, a diagnosis). Then write one small way you can support healing instead (rest, hydration, nourishment, boundaries).

Gentle Breath Reset: Inhale deeply for four counts, exhale slowly for six counts. Imagine you are exhaling the weight of management and inhaling the hope of healing.

Reflection Questions:

- Where have I been numbing or masking instead of listening?
- What is one signal my body has been trying to send me?
- How would it feel to treat my body as an ally instead of an enemy?

Journal Prompts

1. Write about a time you felt betrayed by your body. What truth could reframe that moment?

____

____

2. In what ways has your body carried trauma for you?

____

____

3. What is one belief about your body you're ready to let go of?

____

____

CHAPTER FOUR

Identity Reclaimed (Part One)

Lie: You matter if.
Truth: You matter because you are.

Declaration

I am not my roles.
I am not my weight.
I am not my productivity.
I am who God says I am—loved, worthy, chosen.
I reclaim my name and my voice.
I choose truth over performance and identity over applause.
Today, I live from who I am.

* * *

For most of my life, I was introduced by my roles.

In a small town, family trees arrive before you do. Names are shorthand; lineage is identity. When I walked into a room, I wasn't just Monica—I was "so-and-so's daughter" or "the granddaughter of so-and-so." Later, after I married, I became someone's wife. When my children were born, I became someone's mother.

It wasn't malicious. It was just the way people connected dots in a place where everyone knew each other's stories. But repetition has power. After years of hearing my introductions translated through someone else's name, I absorbed a message: Who I was mattered mostly in relation to who I belonged to.

By the time I was in elementary school, I had already learned the rules: Be the good girl, the good student, the helpful one. Don't rock the boat. Don't ask too many questions. Because asking questions often led to punishment or consequences. I figured out quickly that compliance was safety. Obedience was belonging. The reward for being "good" was that people praised me, and the punishment for questioning was that they reminded me of who I was, as if to say, *Don't ruin the reputation.*

I was the third generation of my family on both sides to live in that town. Our name wasn't just a name—it carried weight. My father managed one of the largest stores in the area, which made him one of the largest employers. He held trust at a level most people never knew—he was privy to the personal lives of his employees in ways only a long-term, deeply respected employer could be.

But trust always comes at a cost. Doing the right thing sometimes made him enemies. Decisions he made as an employer—decisions rooted in fairness, or accountability, or integrity—were occasionally taken out on me at school by teachers or students who didn't like him. Our name was both shield and target.

In my family, it was silently understood that your name was your bond, and your word meant everything. Nobody needed to say it out loud—it was implied in every story told around the dinner table, every expectation placed on me in the community, every glance when I walked into a room. I lived like I carried that name on my back every time I left the house. It meant achievement had to be spotless. It meant mistakes weren't private; they echoed through a town that never forgot. It meant my behavior wasn't just mine—it reflected on an entire family.

So I leaned into the only option that felt safe: Be excellent, be quiet, be reliable. I became the good girl, the one who made teachers proud, the one who helped instead of hindering, the one who never gave anyone an excuse to question my family's reputation. On the outside, it looked like maturity. On the inside, it was survival.

As I grew older, the pattern followed me. In my marriage, I carried roles like a uniform. Not because I was the only one capable, but because responsibility quietly defaulted to me when it was not consistently taken up by my partner.

The only place where I wasn't introduced through my family was work. There, I was Monica, the administrator, the reliable worker, the one who could make chaos behave. But even that identity was laced with performance.

I wasn't just an administrator—I was patient-facing, standing in the middle of life-and-death stakes. The patients I worked with were critically ill pediatric cancer and heart patients. Parents would look me in the eye, desperation etched into their faces, and wait for my answer. My actions dictated whether their child's treatment would be covered by insurance or delayed. Every escalation, every case, carried that weight.

The pressure was relentless. Several times a day, I had to pivot, think outside the box, fight for approvals, and solve problems that could have devastating consequences if I failed. Failure meant chemo delayed. Failure meant a heart device denied. Failure meant a family losing precious time.

My employer never framed it this way—they were always grateful for my work. But I felt it in my bones: Failure was not an option.

The irony was that I received praise for my role. Colleagues admired my dedication. Parents thanked me with tears in their eyes. Supervisors valued my persistence and creativity. From the outside, it looked like I was thriving. But inside, the weight of responsibility pressed down harder and harder.

Every time I pulled off a win, I felt temporary relief—followed immediately by the next crisis. Every "thank you" was a reminder that if I failed tomorrow, the gratitude wouldn't save me. That's the insidious nature of performance-based identity: The applause feels good, but it's never enough to silence the fear that you'll drop the ball next time.

My professional role reinforced the lie I had learned as a child: *You matter if.* You matter if you perform. You matter if you keep it together. You matter if you save the day.

Roles can be beautiful. They give structure and belonging. But they also make convenient armor. Mine looked noble on paper—wife, mother, caregiver, employee—but inside those titles, I went missing. Every compliment for "holding it all together" landed like a brick on a stack I was already struggling to carry. I smiled and said thank you while quietly wondering if anyone could see me underneath the usefulness.

When my health collapsed, I leaned harder into those roles. Structure felt safer than stillness. If I kept moving, I didn't have to hear the questions waiting in the quiet: *Who are you when no one needs you? Who are you when you stop performing? Who are you if the applause never comes?*

I didn't have answers. I had a mask.

The lie sounded like love at first: You matter because you're dependable. You matter because you can take pain and keep serving. You matter because you never drop a ball. It took me decades to notice the condition buried in that sentence—you matter if.

And "you matter if" will exhaust a woman and call it virtue.

By the summer of 2023, I had begun to climb out of pure survival, but my identity still felt secondhand. That July, I attended a coaching event led by a master life coach who also happened to be the trauma coach I had been working with privately for several months. I went in curious but guarded. Part of me was already researching coaching certifications, circling the idea like it might bite. Another part of me carried a list of polished excuses for why I couldn't succeed:

I don't have the time.
I don't have the credentials.
I'm too old to start over.
What if my body betrays me and I can't show up for clients?

Those excuses sounded rational. Underneath, they were fear dressed up in business casual.

On the second day of the event, my coach called my name and invited me on stage for a live coaching session. My stomach dropped. My heart pounded in my throat. The stage was set with large leather chairs you could sink into, softened lights casting a warm glow. Comfortable, yes—but terrifying when every eye in the room was on me.

My coach walked me up the stairs herself, taking me gently by the arm as if to say, *You can do this.* I sat down in the chair, sinking into it but feeling anything but comfortable. My hands trembled. My chest tightened.

And yet, even in the terror, I trusted her. She had walked me through trauma work privately. She knew the lies I carried, the fears that haunted me. Now she was guiding me through them in public, asking the questions I had been too afraid to face: *What if those excuses weren't true? What if your body wasn't your enemy? What if you could create something new?*

I voiced the excuse that had haunted me most: What if my body fights me? What if I can't show up for a client because I'm sick that day?

She looked me straight in the eye and said words that still echo: "Monica, your client would be more worried that you were okay than about rescheduling a session."

It was such a simple statement, but it cracked me wide open.

For decades, I had believed that if I faltered, everything would crumble. That if I wasn't perfect, I wasn't enough. That failure to perform meant failure as a person. And here was my coach, calmly dismantling that lie in front of an audience.

The tears came hot and fast. Not because her words were complicated, but because they shattered a belief I had carried my entire life.

In that moment, I realized that my humanity didn't disqualify me. My imperfection didn't erase my value. My identity wasn't conditional.

After that moment on stage, something shifted in me.

The excuse I had carried for so long—*what if my body fails me, what if I can't show up*—was exposed for what it really was: fear disguised as responsibility. My coach's words replayed in my head again and again: *Your client would be more worried that you were okay than about rescheduling.*

It reframed everything. For years, I believed worth was earned through flawless consistency, through showing up no matter what it cost me. If I faltered, I believed the people counting on me would walk away. But in that single exchange, I saw that my humanity didn't cancel my identity. My imperfection didn't erase my value.

That event planted a seed, but seeds don't grow overnight. I still wrestled with the old lies. I still caught myself measuring worth in productivity, replaying old introductions in my head: wife, mom, caregiver, employee. But the crack in the foundation was there, and once light gets in, it doesn't leave.

I went home differently. I didn't have a new career overnight or a perfectly defined identity, but I had evidence that the lies weren't the whole story. Evidence that other women connected with my vulnerability more than my performance. Evidence that my value wasn't tied to never faltering, but to showing up authentically.

Not long after, I was invited to speak at an event. It was virtual, but it might as well have been a stadium for how nervous I felt. I sat at my desk, staring at the tiny green light on my camera like it was a jury waiting to hand down a verdict. My notes shook in my hands. My voice wobbled. At one point, I lost my place and stumbled.

But something happened as I kept going. My chest, which had been tight with fear, started to loosen. I realized I wasn't performing. I wasn't managing an image. I wasn't hiding behind a role. I was telling the truth. My story. My words. My voice. And that, I realized, was enough.

When the event ended, I didn't feel the familiar crash that came after years of performance. I didn't feel like I needed to collapse under the weight of holding it all together. Instead, I felt clean. Aligned. Whole.

That day, I learned something critical: When you speak from your identity, you don't burn out the same way you do when you speak from performance. Performance drains. Identity sustains.

Over time, I began to embrace a new truth: My identity is not negotiable. Roles may shift. Titles may change. Applause may fade. But who I am—the core of me—remains.

Identity, I've learned, is what's left when the roles fall silent. It is what God spoke over me before anyone else told me who I should be.

For decades, I had lived under the sentence "you matter if." You matter if you perform. You matter if you serve. You matter if you meet expectations. That sentence nearly destroyed me.

Now, I live by a different one: *You matter because you are.*

That truth has changed how I move through rooms. I don't audition for belonging anymore. I don't scan for approval like oxygen. I don't silence myself to keep the peace. My identity isn't rooted in applause—it's rooted in truth.

That doesn't mean the old lies never knock. They do. Sometimes they show up in familiar disguises: be smaller, be quieter, be useful, and you'll be loved. But now I answer them with evidence. I remember the woman who couldn't climb the stairs and the woman who now hikes. I remember the silence that used to choke me and the microphone I now hold. I remember the God who never asked me to earn breath before He gave it.

Identity isn't a trophy you win. It's a truth you live into.

Today, when people ask who I am, I answer differently. I am a coach. I am a daughter of the King. I am a voice for others who are looking for permission to tell their story and find their truth. I am a miraculous transformation.

Each of those pieces matters. "Coach" is a role I'm honored to carry. "Daughter" is an identity that can't be stripped away. "Voice for others" is a calling that gives purpose to my pain. And "miraculous transformation" is both testimony and trajectory—it's the story of where I've been and the path of where I'm going.

The phoenix has become my symbol, not because I rose once and stayed there, but because rising is a rhythm. The first time I saw a phoenix in Harry Potter, I felt something resonate deep inside me. Here was a creature that walked through fire and came out reborn on the other side. It wasn't destroyed by the flames—it was transformed by them.

That's what my life has been: walking through fire—chronic illness, grief, trauma, silence—and rising again. Ashes are not a verdict; they're part of the cycle. I rose when I told the truth on a stage with shaking hands. I rose when I said no to something that would have earned me applause but cost me myself. I rose when I blessed the woman in the mirror without asking her to earn it first. Rising isn't glamorous; it's faithful.

If you are reading this and feel like you are only a collection of job descriptions held together by obligation and caffeine, hear me: Your roles are not your name. They are important. They are not ultimate. Your worth is not in the weight you carry, the hours you log, or the people who claim you. Your worth is older than all of that.

When you live from identity instead of role, everything shifts. You walk into rooms as yourself, not a resumé. You tell the truth faster. You notice the women who are still scanning the floor for their courage, and you create space for them. You remember what it felt like to need permission, so you offer it freely.

That is the gift of a reclaimed identity—It multiplies.

Teaching: How to Know if You're Living from Roles Instead of Identity

Roles can be meaningful, but they are not identity. If you collapse when the applause stops, feel invisible without a title, fear rest because it feels like failure, or introduce yourself by what you do instead of who you are—you may be living from roles instead of truth.

Your identity is unconditional. You don't have to audition for it. You don't have to earn it. You simply have to reclaim it.

Practices and Reflections

Role Release Exercise: Write down your top three roles on a sheet of paper. Next to each one, complete this sentence: *"Even if I could not do this role tomorrow, I would still be..."* Fill in the blank with truths like loved, chosen, resilient, worthy.

Introduction Reset: This week, introduce yourself without using a role. Don't say what you do or who you belong to. Say your name and one truth about yourself. Notice the resistance and the freedom.

Mirror Identity Blessing: Stand before a mirror, place your hand over your heart, and say aloud: *"I am not my roles. I am who God says I am."* Repeat daily until the words begin to soften the old lie.

Reflection Questions:

- Where have I mistaken usefulness for worthiness?
- In what rooms do I feel most like a role and least like myself?
- What one boundary could help me live more from identity than from performance?

Journal Prompts

1. Write about the first time you felt reduced to a role instead of seen as yourself.

____

____

2. When was the last time you used your voice even though it shook? What did you learn about who you are?

____

____

3. Finish the sentence: "I am ____________________, not because of what I do, but because of who I am."

____

____

CHAPTER FIVE

Grief, Silence, and Speaking Truth

Lie: Grief should be hidden. If you stay quiet, it will hurt less. If you keep moving, no one will notice the cracks.
Truth: Silence doesn't heal grief. Speaking it does.

Declaration

I will no longer bury my grief in silence.
My story matters. My losses matter. My voice matters.
Speaking truth is not weakness — it is the first step to healing.
The lie says grief must be hidden. The truth says grief can be spoken, and in speaking it, I will rise.

* * *

The Loss That Shaped Everything

There are dates you never forget. For me, one of them is the day I lost my son, Michael. His life was brief, yet the impact of his absence has stretched across decades. At the time, I didn't know how to hold space for the pain. I only knew how to tuck it away, to be the strong one, to carry on as if I hadn't been broken open.

We had just come through a scare with my dad — open-heart surgery that left the family raw and waiting — when I found out I was pregnant with Michael. The news felt like a second chance stitched into a season of fear. But pregnancy brought more complications: I was put on light bed rest at around twenty-six weeks for preterm labor and spent days in the hospital on a magnesium drip to stop contractions. I was also diagnosed with gestational diabetes, which meant every bite and every blood sugar check felt like a negotiation for his safety.

I paid close attention to my diet, every bite and every number, because I knew how much was at stake. I tried to be as careful and consistent as possible, determined to do my part to keep him safe. I followed medications and appointments because I knew how easily things could go sideways. We made plans, small hopes — a nursery painted, a life imagined — and we held our breath a little less tightly each week.

Then at thirty-six weeks, labor returned and I ended up needing a C-section because he was breech. We were surprised in the delivery room when the doctor announced: It's a boy. The ultrasound tech had told us to expect a girl, so we had no name picked, no tiny blue blanket waiting, no boy clothes folded in a drawer. In the middle of the chaos and joy, there was a jolt of disorientation and hurried adjustments as nurses and family scrambled to fill in what we hadn't prepared.

At first, everything seemed okay. He cried, we breathed, and we leaned into that shaky relief parents know. But after we returned to the room, a nurse's quiet concern about his breathing took the air out of everything. Pediatricians arrived; faces that had been celebratory grew serious. After midnight, with family gone and the hospital hushed under a winter sky, the pediatricians began talking about transferring him to a hospital with NICU. We were in a small mountain town in the middle of a massive snowstorm — there was no NICU nearby, and transport would be hours away.

When the transport team finally arrived, they told us he was too unstable to fly. They could monitor him; they could try to support him. But there was little else they could do at that moment. No explanation for why his tiny lungs struggled so fiercely. The words came soft and sharp: They could not fix this. They offered me one thing that would become seared in my memory — I could hold him while he took his last breath.

They laid him in my arms. I studied every detail of his tiny face — the delicate curl of his fingers, the slope of his nose, the way his chest rose and fell. I memorized texture and light like someone trying to take a photograph with my skin. It was quiet and peaceful in the way tragedies sometimes are, but it was also full of questions without answers. Later, the coroner's office would tell us that his lungs were underdeveloped for reasons they could not explain. That single line felt both a relief and an ache: relief that there was a medical reason, ache that there was still no meaningful explanation.

We made the decision to donate his heart valves to help other newborns. It felt like the smallest good we could offer out of the ruined. The days that followed are mostly a blur. I don't remember leaving the hospital — the motions of grief created a fog that swallowed routines and details. I remember, painfully, the comments from some people in the weeks after: insinuations that maybe I hadn't been careful enough with my diet, or worse, people criticizing how we handled funeral planning. Some even accused me of wasting their time because they had offered advice and time, and when we chose another option, they grew angry. Those words dug into me, layering shame atop grief, convincing me yet again that I had failed in some way or that I was a burden.

At home, we rarely spoke of him. My daughter was five and, in her own way, folded that loss into life and didn't ask many questions. I went back to running my preschool and daycare, to filling days with other people's needs and routines, as though moving fast enough could keep the hole inside from being noticed. But moving didn't heal. It only taught me how to carry my grief quietly while wearing the familiar mask of competence.

What do you do with a love that has nowhere to go? My answer was silence. I thought if I never spoke of it, maybe it wouldn't crush me.

But silence doesn't erase grief. It buries it alive.

Layered Loss

Michael's death wasn't the only grief I carried in silence. Just a few months later, I became pregnant again with my second son. My body was still healing, my heart was still raw, and I found myself navigating pregnancy in the shadow of fresh loss. His birth brought joy, but also a fragile, watchful fear that never fully left me. One year after he was born, my husband sustained a traumatic brain injury. Overnight, I became a caregiver as well as a mother, holding new life in one arm while trying to piece together the fragments of another.

Decades later, another loss arrived when my father passed away — nearly twenty years after Michael. Each grief was different, but each carried an echo of the first. I grieved the son I lost, the version of my husband that no longer existed, the father whose presence once anchored me. I grieved the future I had imagined — the one where life followed a different script. Each layer of loss added weight, and I kept trying to carry it without ever setting it down.

The world applauded me for being strong. But strength, when it's only silence, corrodes from the inside out.

The Cost of Silence

Grief left unspoken doesn't vanish. It leaks into every part of life. It showed up in my body—in migraines, in fatigue, in weight I couldn't lose. It showed up in my relationships—in walls I built so no one could see how much I was hurting. It showed up in my work, in friendships, in the quiet spaces where I pretended to be fine.

I believed the lie that if I never said his name, if I never admitted the depth of my sorrow, I could somehow outlast it. But the truth is, silence made me a prisoner. My voice stayed locked up, my story stayed half-lived, my heart stayed bound.

I remember seasons where I plastered a smile on my face while my insides screamed. Sundays were especially heavy—music or familiar routines stirred something in me, but instead of lifting me, it reminded me of the emptiness. My thoughts often turned into negotiations: *If I can just get through this day, I'll be better tomorrow.* When tomorrow came, the bargaining repeated itself. Life became less about living and more about survival.

Physically, grief lodged itself in my body. I carried exhaustion like a second skin. I battled headaches that no medication could touch, and joint pain that seemed to flare whenever I suppressed another wave of sorrow. Doctors offered prescriptions, but nothing touched the ache that silence kept alive.

In my relationships, I built walls so high that even those closest to me couldn't see the depth of my pain. I became skilled at small talk, at shifting conversations away from myself. I convinced others — and sometimes even myself — that I was fine. But the truth was that silence cost me intimacy. It kept me from being fully known, and therefore, fully loved.

Breaking the Silence

The first time I spoke Michael's name aloud in public, years had passed. My voice shook, but something in me shifted. It was as if the dam finally cracked, and the grief that had been frozen began to move. Speaking the truth didn't erase the pain, but it transformed it. It gave me back my voice. It gave me back my humanity.

Naming our losses matters. Speaking the truth about them matters. Every time I shared a fragment of my story—whether with a friend, a counselor, or on a stage—the power of silence weakened. And with it, the lie that grief must stay hidden began to lose its grip.

One of the most healing moments came when a close friend looked me in the eyes and simply said, "I don't know your exact pain, but I am here." No comparisons. No platitudes. Just presence. It was a reminder that grief shared is grief softened, and that silence broken is hope restored. Later, I met others who had shared in the same grief, and we found comfort in knowing that we were not alone.

Cultural Silence Around Grief

Our culture doesn't know what to do with grief. We hurry people back to work, change the subject when tears surface, or toss out quick fixes like "everything happens for a reason." Instead of giving grief space, we often demand that it be packaged neatly and hidden away. This made my silence even heavier. I didn't just feel pressure from within—I felt it all around me. The world seemed to say: Don't make us uncomfortable with your pain. And so, I swallowed more than I spoke.

Have you felt that too? The sting of someone comparing your loss to theirs, or brushing it off with a platitude? That cultural silence can convince us that grief has no place. But the truth is, grief is part of being human. Entire traditions and cultures have rituals of mourning because grief needs space. It is not unspiritual. It is deeply human, and deeply necessary.

The Brain and Stages of Grief

Psychologists often describe grief in stages—denial, anger, bargaining, depression, and acceptance. But in real life, these are not neat steps;

they overlap, repeat, and circle back. I cycled through them often on the same day. One moment denying Michael was gone, the next bargaining for a different ending, then sinking into the weight of depression. My brain was trying to make sense of a reality it could not accept.

Neuroscience helps us understand why. The brain is wired to expect patterns. When someone we love is suddenly absent, our neural pathways still anticipate their presence. It takes time—and the active work of grieving—for the brain to begin rewiring those pathways. This is why the grief can feel like a shock again and again. Each acknowledgment of absence is another attempt by the brain to reconcile what is with what was.

Healing doesn't erase those pathways, but it builds new ones alongside them. That is why grief may never fully vanish, but it can soften. By speaking grief aloud, by allowing ourselves to feel it, we help the brain update its map of reality. We teach it that we can hold loss and love in the same breath. And over time, the brain learns that safety and hope are possible again, even in the shadow of loss.

Teaching: Grief Is Not a Weakness

Here's what I've learned: Grief is not a weakness. It is love with nowhere to go. It is the body and soul demanding space for what was lost. And it does not heal in silence. Healing begins when we speak, when we tell the truth about what we've carried.

From a neuroscience perspective, unspoken grief can keep the brain stuck in survival mode. When trauma and sorrow are buried, the amygdala stays hyper-alert, scanning for danger. The nervous system can't distinguish between the memory of loss and a present threat, so it responds with the same flood of stress hormones. Cortisol surges, sleep patterns fracture, and the immune system weakens. Over time, this wears down both mind and body.

But when grief is spoken—when it's named, processed, and witnessed—the brain begins to rewire. Memories that once triggered panic start to integrate into the larger story of who we are. The prefrontal cortex, the part of the brain that makes meaning and helps regulate emotions, begins to quiet the overactive amygdala. Instead of reliving the loss on repeat, we start to carry it with more steadiness. This is why journaling, therapy, mindfulness, and community conversations matter so much: They literally change the way the brain processes pain.

Healing grief is not about forgetting or moving on. It's about creating new neural pathways that allow the memory of love to exist without destroying the present moment. Speaking truth calms the nervous system, telling your body: You are safe enough to feel this now. Over time, safety becomes embodied, and hope becomes possible again.

Silence isolates. Truth connects.
Silence shames. Truth frees.
Silence hardens. Truth softens.

You may not need to tell the world your whole story. But you need to stop hiding it from yourself.

Practices and Reflections

Grief healing is not just about words; it is also about creating rhythms that allow your body and mind to release what they have carried. Here are a few practices to try:

Breath Awareness: Sit quietly, close your eyes, and place a hand on your heart. Breathe in slowly, exhale gently. Repeat until your breath feels steady.

Letter Writing: Write a letter to the person you lost. Say the words you never had the chance to say. You do not have to share it; the act of writing can free the unspoken.

Naming Practice: Speak their name aloud. In journaling or in trusted conversation. Each time you say their name, you remind your brain and heart that their life mattered.

Embodied Release: Take a short walk in nature. As you walk, imagine each step helping you carry grief with less weight. Moving your body tells your nervous system you are safe enough to process.

Ritual of Remembrance: Light a candle, create a small memory box, or set aside an anniversary ritual. These tangible acts remind your mind and body that grief has a place and that remembering is part of healing.

Creative Expression: Try painting, drawing, music, or poetry as an outlet. Sometimes the body can express what words cannot, and creative release can become a safe container for grief.

Movement Practice: Engage in gentle yoga, stretching, or even swaying to music. Movement helps release stored tension and reminds the body it is safe to feel.

Shared Storytelling: Find a trusted person or group and share one memory of your loved one. Speaking their story aloud keeps their memory alive and softens isolation.

Reflection questions which can guide you as you practice:

- What emotions surface when you allow yourself to sit still with your grief?
- Where do you feel grief in your body, and what happens when you breathe into that place?
- Who could be a safe person to share one piece of your story with this week?

Journal Prompts

1. What grief have you carried in silence, hoping it would fade?

   ____

   ____

2. Whose voice or reaction taught you to keep your pain hidden?

   ____

   ____

3. What would it look like to honor your loss by speaking it—even if only to yourself or one safe person?

   ____

   ____

4. How has silence affected your body, your work, or your relationships?

   ____

   ____

5. What small step could you take this week to give your grief a voice?

   ____

   ____

Identity Reclaimed (Part Two)

Lie: Who you are is defined by what you've lost.
Truth: Loss shapes you, but it does not define you. Your identity is still yours to reclaim.

Declaration

I am not my losses.
I am not my labels.
I am not my diagnosis or my role.
I am resilient. I am becoming. I am whole.
The lie says I am defined by what happened to me. The truth says I am defined by how I rise, and by the identity I choose to reclaim every single day.

* * *

Part One of this conversation began back in Chapter Four, where we confronted the lie that worth comes from roles or performance. But loss and trauma can distort identity in a different way—by convincing us that we are forever branded by what we've endured.

After Michael's death, I often felt stamped with an invisible label: *the grieving mother.* People looked at me differently, conversations grew awkward, and I learned to wear that role quietly, even when I wanted to scream that I was still more. I remember standing in the grocery store, someone recognizing me and offering pity in their eyes rather than words. I wanted to disappear, because at that moment, I wasn't Monica the woman, the teacher, the dreamer. I was only Monica, the one whose baby had died. That label clung to me like a second skin.

When an old brain injury flared after a viral infection a year after our second son was born, another label quietly attached itself to me: caregiver. What began as temporary support quickly expanded into managing medications, appointments, and rehabilitation. Friends praised my strength, but inside I felt erased. I was no longer experienced as a partner or an individual; I was treated as a nurse, a manager, someone defined by duty rather than relationship. My voice grew quieter, my needs smaller, and my sense of self fractured further as responsibility remained with me long after the crisis had passed.

Add to that years of chronic pain, fibromyalgia, and exhaustion, and I carried yet another unwanted identity: *the sick one.* Even when I fought to keep showing up, inside I felt reduced to symptoms and limitations. Doctors spoke to me as if my pain were my whole name. Well-meaning people offered advice that made me feel unseen, as though my condition was my personality. Each label layered over the next until I struggled to remember who I had been before loss, illness, and duty wrote their names over mine.

There were moments when I caught glimpses of my real identity trying to break through. When I was with my children, they saw me simply as Mom—the one who read them stories, who made them laugh, who held them when they were scared. When I encouraged another woman walking through her own storm, I felt the spark of my voice carrying truth again. Or when I stood at a mirror, weary but unbroken, and whispered to myself that I was still here. These flashes reminded me that beneath the roles and labels, there was still someone whole.

Reclaiming identity meant wrestling with the tension between what happened to me and who I believed myself to be. I had to ask hard questions: Who am I without the labels? Who am I apart from my losses? Who am I becoming if I allow myself to step outside the boxes that grief and illness built around me? These were not questions answered in a day. They were answered slowly, through choices, boundaries, and the courage to believe that my identity could expand again.

The truth is that while loss becomes part of our story, it does not have to be our whole name. Reclaiming identity means remembering that we are more than our wounds. It means separating *what happened to us* from *who we are becoming.*

In those years, most people said nothing at all. Family, friends, neighbors—silence became the background noise of my life. It wasn't cruelty, but uncertainty. They didn't know what to say, so they said nothing. And that silence felt like another label: *untouchable.* I longed for someone to look me in the eye and acknowledge the weight I was carrying, but instead I learned to tuck it in deeper.

When we moved from the mountains to the city, I hoped it would feel like a fresh start. A chance to leave the old labels behind. But labels are sticky; they follow you. I tried to establish a new life without them, only to feel them creep back in, disguised in new forms. The shame pressed harder—the quiet belief that I had failed to accomplish anything great, that I was constantly grasping for proof of my worth. It echoed old childhood messages that I was never enough and always too much at the same time.

What shifted me was stepping into new rooms for the first time— rooms where people spoke truth, where boundaries were honored, where voices mattered. The first time I set a boundary, the first time I stood on a stage and shared my story, the first time I remembered that my worth was not something to be earned but something I had carried since birth—those moments cracked the old labels. They didn't vanish instantly, but they loosened their grip.

One symbolic act sealed this shift for me. As my body changed, I packed up clothes that no longer fit into box after box. For a moment, I thought I was giving myself permission to slide backward, to return to an identity I had outgrown. Instead, I chose differently. I donated seven large moving boxes of clothes to a local women's shelter. It was more than decluttering—it was a declaration. I would not go back. I would not shrink into old patterns. That act of giving away became an act of reclaiming: proof that my future mattered more than my past labels.

When I began re-entering professional spaces, the old labels tried to follow me through the door. I worried people would only see the mom who had survived loss or the woman with health issues. But slowly, I began to notice something else. When I spoke with authority on a topic I knew well, eyes shifted. People leaned in, not because of what I had survived, but because of what I carried in wisdom and experience. That was a turning point—realizing that my voice could lead, not just explain or defend.

At home, too, the shift was gradual. My children didn't introduce me to others as the mother who had been through hard things; they just called me Mom. They saw me laugh again, set boundaries, and chase goals. Their perspective reminded me that while the world may stick labels on us, those closest to us often just see who we are.

One friend once told me, "You're not your story—you're the way you tell it." That line stayed with me. It reminded me that identity isn't erased by pain; it is refined by how we choose to live afterward.

Podcasting later became another milestone in this reclaiming process. Sitting in front of a microphone, without a label attached to me, I had to hear my own voice in a new way. At first, it felt foreign—was anyone really interested in what I had to say? But as I spoke, shared stories, and offered encouragement, I began to believe my words held weight. The feedback from listeners—messages from women who felt seen, who said, "That was exactly what I needed"—confirmed that my story mattered not because of the labels I carried but because of the truth I was willing to share. Each episode became more than content; it became evidence that I was more than my past. My identity was not fixed in what I had endured but was being continually shaped by the voice I chose to raise.

There were other small, almost invisible victories. I remember the first time I introduced myself in a new space without leading with a role or a label. Just my name, standing on its own. It felt strange, as if people were waiting for me to add a qualifier: mother, wife, caregiver, patient. But I let the silence hold, and for the first time in years, I felt the strength of being seen as myself rather than through a filter.

The first time I had a speaking engagement from a stage was terrifying. By then, I had already spoken at several virtual summits, but standing in front of a live audience was entirely different. Before I went on, I was able to share a few minutes with another speaker in the green room. He was seasoned, confident, and his podcast had actually been one of the voices that inspired me at the very start of my own journey. Talking with him reminded me that I belonged there—that I deserved to be on that stage as much as he did. It was a moment of validation, a quiet confirmation that I was stepping into my purpose.

Boundaries, too, became part of reclaiming identity. At first, they were shaky—saying no to an invitation that drained me, asking for help without apologizing, and carving out time to rest. Each small boundary was a reminder that I was not defined by what I could do for others, but by who I was becoming for myself.

Another milestone came when I said yes to being photographed as part of a coaching event and program I was in. I was nervous, trying to figure out the right outfit and poses that would hide the parts of me I was still uncomfortable displaying. A few months later, I had another opportunity to take photos, this time for business marketing. Each shoot became a little easier until my last one, when I felt like a pro—I even had pictures taken on the beach in a swimsuit. What once felt terrifying had become empowering. I'm still not comfortable doing live videos on social media, but sitting in front of a camera for my podcast has now become second nature. Those photos became proof that I could be seen as I was, without apology, and still stand in confidence.

And then there were the quiet, ordinary victories: being able to shop at regular stores instead of only plus-size sections, buying clothes that fit my body instead of hiding it, and learning to choose outfits that made me feel good rather than invisible. I started getting my hair cut and colored on a regular basis, keeping up with manicures and pedicures as part of my self-care routine. These weren't luxuries—they were ways of telling myself that I mattered, that caring for my body was part of reclaiming my identity. I laughed without guilt again. I planned for the future instead of just surviving the day.

Teaching: From Labels to Living Identity

For years, I let labels take root—*grieving mother, caregiver, sick one.* Each label carried some truth about what I had lived through, but none of them told the whole story of who I was. The more I repeated those names to myself, the more they started to feel like my entire identity. I caught myself introducing my life by what I had lost or what I was managing, instead of by what made me feel alive.

Neuroscience explains why this happens. The brain wires itself around the stories we repeat. If I told myself, "I am broken," my brain learned to look for evidence of brokenness. If I practiced, "I am resilient," my brain began to notice the ways I was enduring and adapting. Identity isn't just a concept—it's a pattern of thought that gets reinforced every day.

Psychology calls this the difference between surface roles and core identity. Roles—mother, caregiver, patient—can change, but core identity is made up of values, strengths, and vision. Trauma and illness may shake the surface, but they cannot erase the core. In fact, research on post-traumatic growth shows that adversity often deepens identity. It can lead to stronger empathy, clearer priorities, and a more authentic sense of self.

For me, reclaiming identity meant noticing when I was shrinking into labels and choosing, even in small ways, to speak a different truth. I started by telling myself out loud, *"I am still here."* Later, it grew into, *"I am resilient. I am worthy of joy. I am more than what happened to me."* They were simple words, but they carved new space in my mind and body. Over time, those truths began to feel more real than the labels.

Reclaiming identity isn't about denying loss. It's about refusing to let loss have the final word. It's about remembering that who we are becoming is always larger than what we've endured.

Neuroplasticity research shows that the brain changes based on repetition and attention. Every time we choose to repeat a truth rather than a label, we reinforce new pathways. Over time, those truths feel less like wishful thinking and more like lived reality. It's like strengthening a muscle—the more often you exercise it, the more natural it becomes. Identity is no different.

Psychologists also remind us that identity is not static; it evolves. Who we are at twenty is not who we are at forty or sixty. Trauma and loss may alter the path, but they don't erase the possibility of growth. In fact, studies of post-traumatic growth highlight how adversity can expand our sense of self, often leading to deeper empathy, stronger boundaries, and new purpose. This flexibility means that labels, even when deeply ingrained, are never the final word.

A practical way to think of it is this: Labels act like weights pressing down, while truth acts like breath lifting you up. The more you practice speaking identity truths, the lighter the weight becomes. Eventually, the balance shifts. The old labels may still whisper, but they no longer control the narrative. You learn to live from the deeper part of yourself—the part that cannot be taken by diagnosis, loss, or anyone else's opinion.

Narrative identity research reinforces this truth. Psychologists have found that the way we tell our story reshapes how we see ourselves. When we shift from telling our story through the lens of loss to telling it through the lens of growth, our brain encodes those new versions as real. This is why practices like journaling, therapy, or even podcasting are powerful—they give us a chance to retell the story in ways that emphasize resilience, meaning, and becoming. Each retelling helps carve new neural pathways, turning survival into strength and silence into voice.

Practices and Reflections

Identity isn't rebuilt in one sweeping decision. It comes back through daily, intentional steps that remind you who you are beyond labels. Here are practices that helped me, and that you can adapt to your own journey:

Label Audit: Write down the labels you've been given (by others or yourself). Circle the ones that feel heavy, outdated, or untrue. Cross them out boldly. Then, on a new page, list three identity truths you want to claim moving forward. Keep them somewhere you can see daily.

Identity Anchors: Create 2–3 short phrases that ground you in your true identity (e.g., *I am resilient. I am worthy of joy. I am still becoming.*). Speak them aloud each morning. The act of hearing your own voice declare truth helps retrain your brain.

Boundary Reset: Notice where old labels push you into over-performance or silence. Choose one boundary you can set this week that honors your true identity instead of the old label. This might mean saying no to something that drains you or speaking up in a space where you normally stay quiet.

Voice Practice: In a private space, say your name out loud followed by a truth about yourself: "I am [name], and I am more than what I've been through." Repeat until it feels less foreign. Over time, this can restore your connection to your authentic voice.

Future-Self Visualization: Close your eyes and imagine yourself five years from now, fully living from your reclaimed identity. What does she wear, how does she carry herself, how does she spend her time? Write down what you see, and let that vision guide your choices today.

Reflection Questions:

- Which labels have I mistaken for my identity?
- What truth feels hardest to believe about myself today?
- How would my daily choices shift if I fully embraced my true identity?

Journal Prompts

1. Write about a time you realized you were more than what
    happened to you. What did that moment teach you about your
    true identity?

    ____

    ____

2. What old identity or label do you feel ready to shed, and what has
    kept you holding onto it until now?

    ____

    ____

3. Write a letter to your future self, five years from today. Describe
    the identity truths you hope she is living out.

    ____

    ____

    ____

    ____

    ____

    ____

    ____

4. What new identity truth are you ready to step into this week, and how will you practice it daily?

____

____

5. How would your relationships change if you stopped leading with roles or labels and started showing up as your authentic self?

____

____

CHAPTER SEVEN

Rising Through Resilience

Lie: Resilience means never breaking.
Truth: Resilience is built in the breaking and rising again.

Declaration

I do not have to be unbreakable to be resilient.

My strength is not in never falling—it is in rising, again and again.

The lie says resilience is about perfection. The truth says resilience is built in the breaking, and in choosing to rise.

* * *

Resilience is one of those words people love to throw around. To some, it means grit and toughness, a refusal to bend no matter what life throws at you. But real resilience—the kind I had to learn—is far less polished. It's messy, imperfect, and often forged in the middle of tears, setbacks, and moments when I thought I couldn't keep going.

I used to think resilience meant holding it all together, wearing the mask of strength, and pushing forward no matter what. I thought resilience meant *Don't break.* But after loss, trauma, illness, and the weight of years carrying labels that weren't mine, I discovered something different. Resilience isn't about never breaking. It's about what you do after the breaking. It's about gathering the shattered pieces and choosing to rise, even when you still feel fractured.

There were mornings when just getting out of bed was an act of resilience. Days when driving myself to yet another doctor's appointment, or sitting in the audience at my first speaking event, felt like victories that no one else could see. Resilience didn't look like a roaring comeback. It looked like small, steady steps that kept me from disappearing into the silence.

I remember seasons when my body screamed with chronic pain. Chronic pain and fatigue made every movement feel heavy, and there were days I didn't know how I would keep up with work, parenting, and caregiving. But I did. Sometimes resilience meant taking a hot shower even when my muscles ached. Sometimes it was showing up to run my preschool when all I wanted was to collapse back into bed. Those weren't glamorous moments, but they were bricks laid into the foundation of resilience.

Resilience also took shape in the way I navigated caregiving after my husband's traumatic brain injury. The endless appointments, the long nights of worry, the unpredictable swings of his recovery—all of it stretched me thin. I couldn't fix what had happened, but I could show up for him and for my children. There were days I felt like I was failing everyone, including myself. Yet looking back, I see that resilience was not in doing it perfectly. It was in enduring the imperfection and still choosing love.

Later, resilience looked like standing on a stage for the first time. My heart raced, my palms sweated, and every inner critic screamed that I wasn't qualified to be there. But I stood. I spoke. And when I walked off that stage, I realized resilience was not about never feeling fear—it was about moving forward anyway.

There were other stages of resilience, too, like sitting in front of a microphone to record my first podcast episode. No one could see my trembling hands, but I knew my voice was shaky. I wondered if anyone would care. But the messages I received afterward reminded me that even shaky voices carry power when they speak truth. Resilience was in pressing record again and again until it felt natural.

Resilience was also tested in parenting. Some nights, I tucked my children in with a smile while holding back tears from the weight I carried. Other nights, their laughter pulled me out of despair and reminded me that joy and pain can coexist. Teaching them how to navigate disappointment, loss, and even small daily challenges forced me to practice resilience out loud. I couldn't just tell them to be strong—I had to model what it looked like to bend, not break.

Over time, resilience became less about survival and more about building again. It meant finding ways to rest, to nourish my body, to lean into community, and to practice speaking the truth instead of swallowing it. It meant saying no without apology, and yes to opportunities that scared me but stretched me forward. Resilience was never about perfection. It was about persistence.

One of the most surprising lessons resilience taught me is that it doesn't happen in isolation. I used to think resilience was about being self-sufficient, carrying the load alone. But the deepest resilience came when I allowed myself to be supported—when friends cooked meals, when mentors reminded me of my worth, when my children's laughter pulled me back into the present. Community became the net that caught me when I fell, and the mirror that reflected strength back to me when I couldn't see it in myself.

Resilience also had to grow in the raw silence of grief. After losing Michael, the world around me moved on quickly. People avoided the topic, unsure what to say, while I carried a weight that never left. At first, I thought resilience meant burying the pain and carrying on, but I discovered that true resilience came when I allowed myself to name my grief and, slowly, to share it. Speaking about him, even through tears, became a way to honor his life and to remind myself that I was still alive, too. Each time I broke the silence, I reclaimed a piece of myself.

Resilience also meant living with the labels that came with my health challenges. When I was diagnosed with Ehlers-Danlos Syndrome years later, it gave a name to the chronic pain I had endured since my youth. For a moment, it felt like another weight, another explanation that threatened to define me. Around the same time, I faced a heart condition that thankfully resolved itself, but it forced me to confront the fragility of my own body. Resilience was choosing not to let those diagnoses become my identity. They were part of my story, but not the whole of it. They taught me to listen to my body, to pace myself, and to claim wellness wherever I could find it.

I saw resilience again in visibility. For years, I avoided being seen—whether in photographs, in clothing that fit my new body, or in moments when I felt exposed. But stepping into photoshoots, even when I was nervous, was an act of resilience. Buying clothes that fit instead of hiding behind oversized layers was resilience. Each time I showed up for my business and allowed myself to be visible, I was strengthening the muscle of resilience. I was telling myself: You don't have to hide to be worthy.

Finally, resilience was tested in reinvention. After years of running my daycare, my career path shifted. I worked in healthcare before our move to the city, then transitioned into a position with a law firm, and later found myself back in healthcare once we settled. Each change demanded flexibility, humility, and persistence. Resilience in those seasons meant adapting quickly, learning new skills, and refusing to believe that my worth depended on a single job title. Every pivot reminded me that resilience is not about staying in one place—it's about carrying your strength with you wherever you go.

Resilience also lived in the small, daily decisions that no one else could see. Prepping meals when I was exhausted, stretching when my body wanted to quit, or choosing to go to bed early instead of numbing out in front of the television were all acts of quiet defiance against the pull of giving up. They didn't look heroic, but they built consistency, and consistency built strength.

Resilience also shaped my relationships. There were people I had to let go of—those who drained me, dismissed me, or kept me tethered to old patterns. Choosing distance felt like a loss at first, but it created space for healthier connections. Over time, I began to recognize which voices lifted me higher and which ones pulled me down. That awareness, and the courage to act on it, was resilience in motion.

Boundaries became another frontier of resilience. For so long, I equated love with over-giving and worth with over-functioning. Saying no felt selfish. But resilience taught me that every no was actually a yes to something truer: my health, my family, my purpose. Each time I set a boundary and held it—even when people didn't like it—I grew sturdier inside.

Resilience also revealed itself in milestones that once felt impossible. Traveling again after years of fearing how my body would hold up. Standing in front of new audiences and sharing my story without shrinking back. Even signing book contracts and launching programs were milestones stitched with resilience, because they required me to believe in a future that pain and loss once told me didn't exist.

Resilience was also woven into my work life. Running my preschool and daycare during those years required me to put on a brave face even when I felt like I was unraveling inside. Children still needed routines, and parents still needed a safe place to bring them. I had no staff to lean on—it was just me, opening the doors each morning and carrying the weight of it all. Some mornings I would sit in my car for a few extra minutes, gathering the energy to step inside. But the moment I opened the door, I chose to show up fully. That choice didn't mean I wasn't struggling; it meant I valued consistency for the kids and their families enough to keep going. In hindsight, those days of holding it together for others were proof of resilience, even when I couldn't recognize it at the time.

Another layer of resilience came as I began stepping into coaching and speaking. At first, my voice trembled and my confidence wavered. I worried constantly about whether I was qualified, whether my story mattered, whether anyone would take me seriously. But each time I spoke—whether on a virtual summit, in a coaching call, or eventually on stage—I chipped away at the lie that resilience had to look polished. In reality, it looked like showing up with shaky hands and a steady heart, and discovering that truth carried more weight than perfection.

Resilience also lived in my body. Losing weight was not just about physical health; it was about reclaiming energy, movement, and the possibility of a new life. Donating boxes of clothes to the women's shelter wasn't only an act of generosity—it was a declaration that I would not return to the patterns that once held me down. Each workout, each healthier meal, each photo shoot where I allowed myself to be seen, became a practice of resilience. I was teaching myself that I didn't have to hide anymore, that I could rise in the body I had fought to heal.

Resilience also showed up in the transitions—like when we moved from the mountains to the city. Starting over meant rebuilding routines, relationships, and identity in a place where no one knew my history. It was both freeing and frightening. I had to learn to carry lessons forward without dragging every old label with me. Each new neighbor, each new community event, was a chance to practice showing up as who I was becoming, not who I had been defined as.

Education and growth became another expression of resilience. Enrolling in new programs and certifications while balancing family life and health challenges felt daunting, but each class completed, each credential earned, reminded me that my story was still unfolding. It was proof that resilience isn't just about getting through the hard moments—it's about investing in the future despite them.

Even in moments of doubt, when shame whispered that I wasn't enough, resilience looked like applying anyway, speaking anyway, writing anyway. It meant choosing to risk failure in order to create possibility. That is the quiet courage of resilience: the choice to keep moving, even when the outcome is unknown.

Teaching: What Resilience Really Means

Resilience isn't a trait some people are born with, and others aren't. It's a skill, a set of practices that can be cultivated. Research shows that resilience grows when we:

- Reframe challenges as opportunities for growth.
- Build supportive connections and allow ourselves to lean on others.
- Practice self-care and restore our bodies after stress.
- Tell new stories about what we've survived and who we are becoming.

From a neuroscience perspective, resilience is tied to neuroplasticity—the brain's ability to adapt and rewire. Every time we recover from a setback, even a small one, we strengthen the brain pathways that help us bounce back more quickly next time. Resilience isn't about ignoring pain. It's about teaching the brain and body: *I can survive this, and I can grow through it.*

Resilience also involves emotional flexibility—the ability to feel deeply without being destroyed by those feelings. When we suppress emotion, the nervous system stays locked in survival mode. But when we process, speak, and release it, the brain integrates the experience into our larger story. This is why resilience often looks like both crying and laughing, grieving and celebrating, breaking and rising—sometimes all in the same day.

From a neuroscience perspective, resilience is supported by the brain's plasticity. Each time we recover from a challenge—whether it's standing up after failure, calming ourselves after a stressful event, or reentering the community after isolation—the brain is literally rewiring. New neural pathways form that make it easier to cope the next time. In this way, resilience is not a single trait but an accumulation of repeated practice.

Research on post-traumatic growth also shows that adversity can lead to greater appreciation for life, deeper relationships, and new possibilities. While trauma can fracture us, resilience is the process of integrating that pain into a larger story where we are not only survivors but also builders of meaning.

Polyvagal theory helps explain why resilience is so tied to the body. When our nervous system is dysregulated by fear or loss, we are thrown into fight, flight, or freeze. But practices like slow breathing, grounding exercises, and safe connection with others signal to the body that we are safe again. Over time, these signals teach the nervous system to recover more quickly, and resilience becomes embodied rather than forced.

You can think of resilience like a muscle: The more it is used, the stronger it becomes. But just like a muscle, it also needs recovery. Strength is built in the cycle of stress and rest, effort and renewal. Real resilience honors both—the rising after the breaking, and the pauses that make the rising possible.

Psychologists describe resilience not only as bouncing back but also as growing forward. Research on emotional agility shows that how we relate to our emotions determines how we adapt. Instead of ignoring fear or grief, resilient people acknowledge them, label them, and then choose actions aligned with their values. This flexibility reduces stress and helps us respond instead of react.

Another way to understand resilience is through metaphor. It is like scar tissue—formed after injury, never quite the same, but often stronger in its repair. It is also like the seasons: Winter may strip life bare, but spring always returns with growth. Resilience honors both the barrenness and the blooming.

Practical practices also support resilience. Gratitude journaling has been shown to shift attention from what is missing to what is present, building optimism. Mindfulness, even a few minutes a day, calms the nervous system and restores perspective. Regular social connection— whether sharing a meal, making a phone call, or joining a group— provides belonging, which is one of the most powerful buffers against stress. Each of these habits may feel small, but together they become the scaffolding that holds us steady in the storms of life.

Teaching Bridge

Resilience doesn't always roar. Sometimes it whispers.
It's in the breath between breakdown and rebuilding—the quiet promise that you'll keep showing up for yourself, one sunrise at a time. Resilience is not about pushing harder or pretending the pain never existed. It's about softening into grace, letting the light back in, and trusting that the same strength that carried you through the storm will guide you into calm.

Every chapter of resilience is written in real life—not the highlight reels, but the everyday moments of choosing to begin again. That's where the rising truly happens: in the ordinary courage to keep moving forward, even when no one is watching.

Practices and Reflections

Here are some ways to practice resilience:

Micro-Victories: At the end of each day, write down one thing you did that was hard but you did anyway. Celebrate the small wins—they stack up over time.

Rest as Resistance: Build intentional rest into your week. Resilience is not about endless output; it requires refueling.

Connection Check: Identify one safe person you can reach out to this week. Resilience grows in community, not isolation.

Reframe: Write down a recent setback. Then write one way it has stretched you or revealed a strength you didn't know you had.

Embodied Reset: Practice grounding exercises such as deep breathing, stretching, or walking outdoors. These tell your body: *You are safe. You can begin again.*

Reflection Questions:

- When have I mistaken "resilience" for overworking or over-functioning?
- Where am I being called to rest so that I can rise stronger?
- Who can I lean on this week instead of carrying everything alone?
- What small act of resilience did I show today that I want to celebrate?

Journal Prompts

1. Describe a time you thought you couldn't rise, but you did. What helped you take that step?

____

____

2. Write about a current challenge you're facing. How can you reframe it as part of your growth?

____

____

3. What does true resilience look like for you—not the polished version, but the lived one?

____

____

4. How do you want to define resilience for the next chapter of your life?

____

____

5. Who has modeled resilience for you, and what did you learn from their example?

____

____

CHAPTER EIGHT

The Phoenix Rises

Lie: I have to keep surviving to stay strong.
Truth: True strength is found in choosing to rise — not just survive.

Declaration

I am not defined by what I've lost or by what burned away.
I am defined by how I rise, rebuild, and live with purpose.
The fire refined me. The ashes grounded me.
And now, I rise—brighter, bolder, and freer than before.
Each breath I take is proof of renewal. Each choice I make is part of my legacy.
I am the phoenix. I am the flame. I am the rise.

* * *

The car was quiet except for the low hum of the engine and the rhythm of my own breath. I remember staring through the windshield, watching raindrops slide down in streaks of silver. The world outside was muted and gray. Inside, I felt hollow—like everything that once defined me had been burned to ash. My body ached, my spirit was weary, and my faith in what was next flickered like a dying ember. Grief, illness, exhaustion, and disappointment had piled so high that I couldn't see anything beyond survival. I was alive, but I wasn't living.

There were days my body felt like it was made of smoke—heavy, shifting, impossible to hold together. The exhaustion was bone-deep, the kind that sleep couldn't fix. I remember lying awake at night, my thoughts restless, my soul pleading for something—anything—that felt like hope. Even simple things like taking a shower or making dinner felt like climbing a mountain barefoot. I had nothing left to give, but the world kept asking for more. My reflection in the mirror was a stranger—eyes dull, shoulders tense, heart guarded. I looked alive on the outside, but inside I was unraveling.

In that moment of stillness, I didn't know I was sitting in one of the most sacred spaces of my story—the ashes. The place between endings and beginnings. The space where everything familiar falls away, and something new is quietly waiting to emerge. Years earlier, I had read about the phoenix in a *Harry Potter* book—a mythical bird that bursts into flame, dies, and then rises from its own ashes. I was captivated by it then but never understood why. It was just a story... until that night, when the memory surfaced like a whisper from somewhere deep within me. The image of that bird rising through the smoke burned itself into my mind, and I suddenly knew: This was my ashes moment.

The years leading up to that night had been fire upon fire—losing Michael, watching the dreams I had built for my family crumble, battling chronic illness and pain that no medication could fix, and carrying the invisible weight of being the strong one while silently unraveling inside. The fire stripped everything familiar from me—my identity, my health, my sense of control. But what I didn't realize then was that the fire wasn't there to destroy me. It was refining me.

Fire has a way of revealing what's indestructible. When everything external burned away—the expectations, the comparisons, the need to prove—I was left face-to-face with the truth of who I was. Not the version the world expected. Not the woman performing strength. But the one who remained when there was nothing left to lose.

The rising didn't happen all at once. It began with a flicker—tiny acts of defiance against despair. A walk outside when my body screamed for rest. A prayer whispered when words failed me. Choosing to eat, to rest, to breathe through another day. Those small, steady choices fanned the ember back into flame. There wasn't a dramatic revelation—just a quiet clarity one morning, a whisper that said, *"You can't live here anymore."* I didn't even know where "here" was at that point, only that I was meant for something beyond it. Rising wasn't about fighting the fire anymore; it was about stepping out of it. That whisper became my turning point—the moment I realized rising wasn't a single act; it was a practice. One small act of courage, one breath, one truth at a time.

As I rebuilt, I learned that survival and rising are not the same. Survival is reactive—it's doing whatever it takes to get through the fire. Rising is intentional—it's deciding what to build once the smoke clears. I had spent so many years surviving that I forgot what it meant to live with vision. But healing pulled me toward something deeper. I didn't want to rebuild what had burned; I wanted to create something new— something rooted in purpose.

The first true spark of rising came the day I chose to stop hiding behind my pain. For years, I had carried my story quietly, afraid of judgment, afraid that speaking it aloud would make the pain real again. But one day, I felt a nudge—a quiet but persistent voice urging me to share. I told my story for the first time in a small group, my voice trembling, my heart pounding. And when I finished, something miraculous happened. No one looked away. No one judged. Instead, I saw recognition in their eyes—the same kind of pain, the same kind of resilience. At that moment, I realized my ashes could light the way for someone else. My survival had become a bridge to healing for others.

Healing doesn't announce itself—it hums softly in the background. It was in those quiet mornings when I noticed I could breathe without bracing, when the tears that used to come daily now came less often. I would step outside and feel sunlight warming my face, and for the first time in years, it didn't feel harsh—it felt like grace. I remember watching a bird lift off from a fence post, its wings slicing through the air, and thinking, *maybe I can do that too.* That was grace in the middle—before the full rise, before the success stories or breakthroughs—just the subtle recognition that I was still here, and that was enough. Each breath, each sunrise, each quiet moment of gratitude became evidence that I was coming back to life.

I started to feel strength returning—not the brittle strength of endurance, but the soft, steady strength of peace. The rising didn't look like fireworks or applause. It looked like sunlight through the blinds after another long night. It looked like laughter that felt foreign at first but eventually became familiar. It looked like mornings when my body still ached, but I got up anyway—not because I had to, but because I wanted to. That's how I knew I was no longer surviving. I was rising.

Eventually, the phoenix became more than a symbol—it became a mirror. I saw myself in its cycle: burning, breaking, resting, and rising. Every time I thought I had reached my limit, another layer of transformation began. I realized that the rising never truly ends; it just changes form. Some seasons call for soaring, others for stillness—but both are sacred. The fire taught me that beginnings often wear the disguise of endings, and rebirth doesn't erase the ashes—it builds upon them.

There was a day I came across an image of a phoenix again—fiery wings outstretched, gold and crimson feathers glowing against a dark sky. This time, it wasn't just beautiful. It was personal. It was me. I started noticing the phoenix everywhere: in jewelry, artwork, even in conversations that felt divinely timed. Eventually, it became the emblem of everything I believed in. When I sat down to design my business and create a symbol that represented my story, there was never any question. The phoenix had followed me through every stage of loss and renewal. Choosing it was not a branding decision—it was a soul decision. It carried the message I wanted every woman I worked with to feel: that she, too, could rise. Every time I saw that golden bird, it reminded me of my vow—to live a life that honored the ashes, not hid from them.

Looking back, I see that the phoenix didn't just find me—it followed me. It waited patiently until I was ready to understand. It whispered through every storm: *You can rise again.* And I did. Over and over. The woman I am now carries both the fire and the flight—the ache and the awakening. My ashes are no longer a graveyard; they are the foundation of everything I've built.

That's what rising truly is: taking the story that nearly destroyed you and turning it into something that sets others free. Choosing to live, not in spite of the fire, but because of it. The phoenix reminds me every day that strength is not about staying untouched by the flames— it's about trusting the fire to reveal what was eternal all along. And that is how I learned to rise.

The Body's Memory of Fire and Flight

My body had always remembered the fire—tight chest, shallow breath, the instinct to brace. Rising meant teaching it to trust peace again. Each deep breath became an act of defiance, each stretch of movement a reminder that I could move without pain or fear. Slowly, I stopped holding my shoulders like armor and began to walk with a sense of ease. My body became my proof of resilience—an echo of the storms it had survived and the strength it carried within. Learning to feel safe inside myself was one of the purest forms of healing.

The more I embodied peace, the more my mind followed. My breath deepened, my sleep steadied, and my energy shifted from surviving to thriving. The fire had once been my identity; now it was only my story. My body no longer flinched quietly. It had learned that calm was safe.

The Ripple Effect: Rising Inspires Others

Rising didn't stay contained within my own life. It began to spill outward. A friend mentioned that she finally scheduled a doctor's appointment she'd been avoiding. A client wrote to tell me she started journaling again after hearing my story. My daughter told me she noticed I laugh more now. The energy of rising is contagious—it gives permission. I realized that my healing wasn't meant to end with me; it was meant to flow through me. Every time I showed up authentically, I created space for others to do the same. That is the legacy of the phoenix—not to prove endurance, but to ignite hope.

The Sacred Ordinary: The Daily Rise

Most days, rising doesn't roar. It hums. It looks like brewing tea in the morning, taking a deep breath before a busy day, or pausing long enough to notice sunlight through the trees. Rising became the rhythm of my everyday life—a practice of presence rather than perfection. Some days, I still feel the ashes under my feet, but they no longer weigh me down. They remind me of how far I've come. The fire forged me, but peace sustains me.

Teaching: The Psychology of Rising

Rising is not simply about endurance; it's about transformation. Survival gets you through the night, but rising teaches you how to live again. It's the moment you shift from reacting to life to intentionally creating it. After years of living in survival mode, the body and brain adapt to constant stress. The nervous system becomes wired for danger, scanning for what might go wrong instead of trusting what could go right. The first step in rising is teaching your body that peace is not the absence of motion—it's the foundation for it.

From a psychological perspective, rising mirrors what researchers call *post-traumatic growth*. It's the process of not only recovering from pain, but finding deeper meaning through it. After a loss, the brain seeks to make sense of chaos. When we begin to assign meaning—to see purpose within pain—we rewire the brain's pathways toward resilience and hope. That's why storytelling, reflection, and community are such powerful tools in healing. They remind us that our stories are not endings. They are evolutions.

Rising is also cyclical. There's the fire—the stripping away of what no longer serves you. There's the ashes—the stillness, the surrender, the quiet grief. Then there's the rise—the rebuilding, the reclaiming, the rebirth. And eventually, the cycle repeats. Each rise leaves you stronger, softer, and more self-aware. You begin to see that there is no single moment of becoming. There is only the continual rhythm of rising.

On a spiritual level, rising is an act of surrender. It's the moment you stop asking, *"Why me?"* and begin asking, *"What now?"* It's trusting that even the ashes have a purpose—that every ending clears space for something greater. Rising doesn't require perfection; it requires willingness. Willingness to believe that the fire didn't happen to destroy you but to refine you. Willingness to hold both pain and possibility in the same breath. Willingness to begin again, even when the outcome is uncertain.

When you rise, you shift from survival to legacy. You start to make decisions not out of fear, but from vision. You begin to see how your healing impacts the people around you. Rising is contagious—it sparks permission in others to do the same. The woman who rises doesn't need to announce it; her presence says it for her. Her peace becomes proof that transformation is possible.

And like the phoenix, rising requires both burning and rest. The fire clears. The ashes ground. The flight begins only after the rebuilding. It's not about rushing the process; it's about honoring every part of it. When you learn to trust your own timing, you stop comparing your pace to anyone else's. You begin to understand that resilience is not about moving quickly—it's about moving intentionally.

Every time you rise, you're building neural pathways of strength and confidence. The brain learns through repetition: Each moment you choose peace instead of panic, hope instead of despair, authenticity instead of performance, you're training yourself to rise faster and softer the next time. Rising becomes muscle memory.

3 Ways to Honor Your Own Rising

1. Rest Without Guilt:
Rest is not the opposite of growth—it's part of it. The phoenix doesn't rise until it has rested in the ashes. Give yourself permission to pause without shame.

2. Tell the Truth of Your Story:
Speak your story out loud, even if your voice trembles. Naming your experience releases the power it holds over you. When you share, you transform pain into purpose.

3. Live From Vision, Not Fear:
Ask yourself, "What am I building toward?" rather than "What am I avoiding?" Living from vision is how survival turns into legacy. It's how the ashes become fertile ground for new growth.

Practices and Reflections

From Awareness to Embodied Change

Insight without practice fades. This chapter is not meant to stay in your head. It is meant to move into your body, your choices, and your daily life. The practices below help you shift from knowing to becoming.

Take these slowly. One practice done consistently is more powerful than doing them all once.

Grounding Practice: Name What Is True Right Now

Before change, there must be truth.

Sit with your feet on the floor. Place one hand on your chest and one on your belly. Take three slow breaths, in through your nose, out through your mouth.

Quietly name:

- One thing you feel in your body
- One emotion present right now
- One truth you are avoiding but already know

No fixing. No judging. Just noticing.

This practice teaches your nervous system that awareness is safe.

Body-Based Practice: Interrupt the Pattern

When you notice yourself slipping into an old response pattern, pause and do the following:

- Press your feet firmly into the ground.
- Name out loud what is happening: "I am feeling overwhelmed."

- Choose one small regulating action: a walk, water, breath, or stretching.

You are not failing. You are practicing interruption. That is progress.

Faith and Trust Practice: Release Control, Reclaim Alignment

If faith is part of your life, or if you believe in a higher wisdom beyond yourself, try this reflection.

Place your hands open in your lap. Take a slow breath.

Say quietly or internally:

"I release what I was never meant to carry alone. I choose trust over control."

If faith language does not resonate with you, replace it with:

"I do not need to force clarity. I allow it to unfold."

Notice what softens.

Reflection Questions:

Answer these honestly. Write without editing yourself.

- What pattern or behavior keeps repeating in my life, even though I say I want change?
- What does this pattern protect me from feeling or facing?
- When I imagine letting this pattern go, what fear immediately rises?
- What would it look like to choose progress instead of perfection in this area?
- What is one small, embodied action I can take this week that supports who I am becoming?

Identity Reflection: Who Are You Becoming

Complete these sentences without overthinking:

- I am learning to trust myself when I _______________________.
- I am no longer available for _______________________.
- The version of me I am becoming values ________over________.

Let this reflection anchor your next steps.

Closing Integration

You do not need a dramatic breakthrough. You need consistent truth, gentle regulation, and aligned action.

This work is not about fixing yourself.

It is about remembering who you are when the noise quiets.

Choose one practice. Return to it daily for the next seven days.

That is how change takes root.

Journal Prompts

1. What has been your greatest "fire" moment—the one that felt like everything was falling apart? What did it reveal or refine in you?

   ____

   ____

2. Where in your life are you still living in survival mode? What might rising look like instead?

   ____

3. What symbols or reminders—like the phoenix—help you stay grounded in your own strength?

____

____

4. When was the last time you noticed your own progress, even if it was small? How can you celebrate that rise today?

____

____

5. How might your story of rising give permission for someone else to heal?

____

____

CHAPTER NINE

Becoming Her – The Rebirth

Lie: Healing means going back to who I was.
Truth: Healing transforms you into who you were always meant to be.

Declaration

I am not who I was and I do not need to be.
Every ending in my story was preparing me for this becoming.
The woman I am today carries the wisdom, grace, and strength of every version I have been.
This is my rebirth.
This is me becoming her.

* * *

There is a moment in every rebirth when the ashes are still warm. The smoke is lifting, the air is heavy with what was, and yet—somewhere in that stillness—a spark catches. It's quiet, but it's undeniable. That spark is *you*, waking up to the truth that you were never meant to return to who you were before the fire. You were meant to rise as someone new.

For me, becoming her—the woman I am now—wasn't one defining moment. It was a thousand small ones. It was the morning I looked in the mirror and, for the first time, didn't see everything I had lost. It was the moment I realized that peace didn't mean life was easy; it meant I no longer needed to fight myself. It was stepping on stage, sharing my story, and realizing I no longer needed validation to prove I belonged there. I had become her long before I noticed. The fire had done its work. The ashes had settled. I had risen.

Becoming her required shedding identities that once felt safe. The caregiver. The survivor. The woman who had to earn her worth through service, perfection, or pain. Each role had protected me at one time, but they weren't built for who I was becoming. Letting them go felt like grief, but it was actually grace. I had to make peace with the version of me who carried me this far, while trusting that a new version was waiting to emerge.

There was a time I believed healing meant restoration—that I would somehow go back to the woman I was before the trauma, the loss, the illness. I now know healing is not a return. It's a reconstruction. The old foundations crack, and the new ones are poured by hand, one intentional act at a time. Each boundary, each breath, each decision to stay instead of run was another brick in the woman I was building.

In that rebuilding came identity. I learned that becoming her was less about discovering something new and more about remembering what had always been there—buried beneath obligation, comparison, and fear. I stopped asking, "Who am I now?" and began asking, "Who have I always been beneath the noise?" The answer came slowly: strong, intuitive, faithful, worthy. Not because of what I achieved, but because of who I decided to be.

For years, I measured my growth by what I could *do*. How much I could handle. How much I could give. But becoming her wasn't about adding more; it was about releasing what didn't belong. It was learning to be at home in my own skin, to make peace with stillness, to stop waiting for permission to live. There's a sacred power in realizing that survival is not the same as living. Healing taught me the difference.

Becoming her looked like rediscovering joy without guilt. Dancing in the kitchen again. Laughing too loud. Saying 'yes' to things that scared me and 'no' to things that drained me. It looked like choosing rest without shame. Wearing color again. Taking up space in conversations, on stages, in rooms, I once shrank myself to fit. Each moment was a declaration: I am not returning—I am becoming.

And with each new layer of becoming came another kind of shedding. The opinions of others. The timelines I thought I had to meet. The silent pressure to be palatable, polished, or perfect. The woman I was becoming didn't need to prove anything. She was rooted, not restless. She had traded striving for surrender and people-pleasing for peace.

It wasn't an instant transformation—it was slow, sacred evolution. It came with setbacks, doubt, and moments when I wanted to retreat into the familiar. But each time, I remembered the fire. I remembered that the ashes were evidence of what I'd survived. And I chose, again, to rise.

Becoming her also revealed itself in the ordinary rhythms of daily life. It was choosing gentleness when I once would have chosen guilt, asking for help instead of hiding, trusting my intuition instead of second-guessing it. It was showing up for work, for family, for myself, with a quiet steadiness that didn't need to prove anything. Becoming her wasn't glamorous—it was grounded. It happened in the pauses, in the moments between doing and being, where peace finally felt like home.

Community and mentorship also became mirrors of my becoming. I found strength in conversations with women who had walked their own fires and come out shining. Their honesty reminded me that I wasn't alone, and their courage helped me find mine. Mentors offered wisdom when I couldn't see the bigger picture, and friends held space for my growth without trying to fix it. Together, we reminded each other that transformation doesn't require perfection—it requires presence.

And then, there was the sacred fire itself—the symbol that has always spoken to me. The phoenix doesn't rise untouched; it rises renewed. The ashes aren't a mark of failure; they're evidence of the refining. The fire stripped away everything false and revealed what was eternal: strength, truth, and purpose. I no longer feared the flames because I knew what they created. Every ending had simply been a beginning in disguise, and I had finally learned to trust the burn.

Becoming her showed up in unexpected moments. It was walking into a room and not shrinking. It was hearing my voice on a recording and not flinching at its sound. It was sitting in silence without needing to be filled. These weren't grand transformations—they were quiet recognitions that I had become comfortable with myself. For the first time in my life, I didn't need to be performing. I could simply be.

There was a morning when I woke up and realized I hadn't thought about the past version of myself in weeks. The ache that once followed me had softened. The mirror no longer reflected a woman trying to prove her worth; it showed a woman standing in it. I wasn't chasing approval anymore—I was walking in alignment. That realization felt like freedom, not fireworks. It was subtle, steady, and sacred.

Becoming her also meant learning how to rest without guilt. I used to believe productivity was proof of purpose. That if I wasn't constantly striving, I was somehow slipping backward. But healing taught me that peace can be just as productive. Some of my greatest growth happened in stillness—on quiet evenings when I sat with a cup of tea, journaling, reflecting, breathing. Those pauses used to make me anxious; now they have become a reminder that I am safe.

One of the most powerful indicators of becoming was my first in-person speaking event after years of doing virtual talks. I remember standing backstage, the lights warm against my face, the hum of the crowd just beyond the curtain. Old patterns of doubt whispered that I wasn't enough, that someone else would do it better. But then, a deeper voice rose within me—the voice of the woman I had become. She reminded me that I wasn't there to impress anyone. I was there to serve, to share, to stand in truth. When I stepped on that stage, it didn't feel like a performance; it felt like a purpose. I spoke from peace, not pressure, and that was the difference.

The woman I was before the fire needed external validation to feel seen. The woman I am now knows that visibility is an inside job. My worth doesn't rise and fall with applause—it's anchored in truth. Every time I share my story, every time I show up authentically, I reinforce that truth a little more. Becoming her wasn't about perfection; it was about presence.

And it's not that fear disappeared—it just lost its authority. I still have moments when doubt tries to sneak in, when old stories whisper that I should play small. But now I recognize those thoughts for what they are: echoes from a chapter I've already closed. Fear may visit, but it no longer gets to lead. The woman I've become knows how to hold fear in one hand and faith in the other and move forward anyway.

Becoming her means I no longer rush my healing or my growth. I trust the timing. I trust myself. I no longer apologize for being too much or for wanting more. I've learned that wholeness doesn't mean having everything figured out; it means embracing every version of myself— the broken, the brave, and the blooming. That is the rhythm of rebirth: to honor the ashes and still choose to rise again, softer but stronger, steady but on fire with purpose.

Teaching: The Psychology of Becoming

Healing and becoming are two sides of the same process. Healing restores safety; becoming restores identity. When you've lived in survival mode for years, your nervous system learns to equate chaos with comfort. The first step toward becoming her is teaching your body that peace is safe.

From a neuroscience perspective, every act of healing reshapes your brain's wiring. This process, called neuroplasticity, means that your thoughts and choices are literally carving new pathways—pathways that make calm, confidence, and joy more accessible over time. Healing begins in the nervous system; becoming happens when those new pathways start to feel like home.

Psychologically, becoming is an integration. It's when all the fragments of your story begin to make sense together. The parts you once rejected—your pain, your mistakes, your vulnerability—become the foundation of your power. You no longer define yourself by what happened to you, but by how you chose to grow through it.

Becoming her also means allowing space for rest and curiosity. Growth doesn't always look like progress on paper. Sometimes, it looks like stillness—listening inward instead of pushing forward. That's where alignment takes root. The woman you are becoming is not in a rush. She trusts the timing of her own becoming.

True becoming is not about creating a new identity out of thin air; it's about remembering who you are beneath the noise. It's about integration, not invention. The mind begins to follow what the heart already knows: that you are whole, worthy, and capable of joy right now. As you practice embodying this truth, your thoughts, emotions, and actions begin to align. That alignment is where transformation becomes sustainable.

Becoming is both science and spirit. The brain rewires through repetition, but the soul rewires through surrender. When you stop forcing outcomes and begin trusting the unfolding, peace replaces striving. It's not passive; it's powerful. Faith, in whatever form it takes for you, becomes the bridge between who you've been and who you're becoming.

This process is not linear. You may revisit old patterns, question your progress, or doubt your strength. That doesn't mean you're failing; it means you're evolving. Every cycle brings deeper awareness and stronger alignment. Like layers of the earth forming over time, each season of becoming leaves you more grounded, more centered, and more sure of your truth.

The 5 I's of Becoming (Simplified Overview)

These five pillars offer a simple rhythm for navigating transformation:

Intention: The decision to rise. Every shift begins with a conscious choice to no longer live from old patterns.

Integration: The work of bringing your inner healing into your daily life—aligning how you think, act, and relate.

Identity: The remembering. This is where you begin to embody the truth of who you've always been beneath fear and conditioning.

Integrity: Living in alignment with your values, even when it's uncomfortable. Choosing truth over approval, peace over performance.

Illumination: The expansion. As you live from alignment, your life becomes a light for others without forcing it. Your presence itself becomes proof of what's possible.

Each "I" builds on the last, creating a rhythm rather than a rigid system. These concepts are a glimpse into the deeper work I share in my coaching and live events—practices that invite you to live in harmony with the woman you're becoming, not just think about her.

Closing Reflection

Becoming her isn't a finish line; it's a lifelong unfolding. Every version of me that came before this moment still lives within me, not as baggage but as wisdom. The woman who survived the fire gave me grit. The one who learned to rest taught me grace. The one who dared to rise taught me faith. Each layer carries its own strength, and together they form the whole. That's the beauty of becoming—it never asks you to erase your past. It invites you to integrate it.

There's a sacred peace that comes when you realize the woman you were searching for was never missing—she was waiting. Waiting for permission to be seen, to be felt, to lead. Waiting for you to remember that healing doesn't make you someone new; it allows you to return to the truest version of yourself. The becoming is not about striving; it's about remembering. It's the quiet confidence that says, "I am home within myself."

Becoming her is not about perfection or arrival. It's about presence. It's waking up each day and choosing to live as the woman you promised yourself you would be. It's trusting that the same fire that once burned you also refined you. It's looking at the ashes of what once was and saying, "Thank you for making room for more."

And as I stand here—no longer trying to rebuild what was lost but building what is meant to be—I understand that the fire was never the end of my story. It was the beginning of my becoming. And perhaps that's the gift we all share: the power to rise, to rebuild, and to become.

Practices and Reflections

The Mirror Moment: Stand in front of a mirror, look into your eyes, and say out loud, *"I am not who I was. I am becoming who I am meant to be.*" Notice what emotions surface. They are invitations to deeper healing.

Release Ritual: Write down the identities, labels, or beliefs that no longer fit—things like *caretaker*, *perfectionist*, *not enough*. Burn or bury the paper as a symbolic act of release. Make space for the new.

Embodiment Practice: Choose one action each day that aligns with your future self. It could be dressing with confidence, resting without guilt, or speaking up in a meeting. Small, consistent actions build identity.

Reflection: Write about one part of your story you've always tried to hide. What strength did that experience reveal in you? How can you honor it as part of your becoming?

The Joy Practice: Schedule something purely for pleasure this week—music, laughter, nature, movement. Healing deepens when joy returns.

Journal Prompts

1. When did you realize you were no longer the woman you used to be?

____

____

2. What version of you have you outgrown and what version is emerging?

____

____

3. What emotions come up when you think about letting go of who
    you once were?

    ____

    ____

4. How do you want to define *becoming* in this next season of your
    life?

    ____

    ____

5. What does your "rebirth" look and feel like?

    ____

    ____

CHAPTER TEN

Legacy Rising

Lie: My story ends with me.
Truth: My story is the spark that lights the way for others.

Declaration

I am a living legacy in motion.
My story is not finished—it's expanding.
Every time I rise, I light the path for another.
I carry the flame of transformation with courage and grace.
I am not waiting to leave a legacy.
I am living it now.

* * *

I remember the room—the soft hum of voices, the nervous laughter, the weight of a hundred stories waiting to be told. The space felt warm and safe, lit with the glow of soft lamps and the faint scent of coffee. The stage held two leather chairs and a fluffy rug that made the room feel more like a living room than an event space. It was intimate, cozy, and alive with anticipation. I sat at a round table with several women, my notebook open, heart pounding quietly beneath my ribs.

The coach, a woman with a calm but commanding presence, walked to the front of the room. She reached into a glass bowl filled with names and drew one out. I tried to steady my breathing as she looked down at the slip of paper, then back up. Her eyes landed on me. She smiled, crossed the room, and gently placed a hand on my arm. "You're up," she said with a grin that was equal parts warmth and challenge. My stomach dropped. For a moment, I wanted to shrink back but something inside whispered, *This is your moment.*

I stood and followed her to the front. The walk to the stage felt longer than it was, a slow-motion moment where time bent. I sank into the leather chair, the soft rug grounding me as I tried to ignore the weight of a hundred pairs of eyes. My palms were damp, my heart hammering in my chest. The coach sat across from me, legs crossed, and smiled. "So," she said, "what's holding you back right now?"

I hesitated, feeling exposed under the warm light. The words caught in my throat, but I forced them out. "I want to become a coach," I said quietly, "But I'm scared. My health still isn't where I want it to be, and I'm afraid I won't be able to show up for my clients. What if I can't give them what they need? What if I fail them?"

The words hung heavy in the air, louder in my own ears than they probably sounded to anyone else. Saying them out loud made the fear real. For a moment, the room was silent except for my shaky breath. Tears pressed at the back of my eyes, that familiar lump in my throat that came whenever I brushed too close to vulnerability.

She nodded, eyes soft with understanding. "You know," she said, "Your clients won't care if you need to reschedule a session. They'll be more concerned about *you.* They'll want to know you're okay."

Her words landed like a gentle shock—simple but profound. My shoulders relaxed, my chest loosening as if I'd been holding my breath for months. I felt tears spill over as I nodded. She continued, "The very thing you think disqualifies you might be the thing that connects you most deeply to them. They don't need perfect. They need real."

In that instant, something inside me shifted. I had spent so long believing that healing had to be complete before I could help others— that I needed to arrive before I could lead. But what if that wasn't true?

What if leadership was born in the middle of the mess, in the rising itself? Maybe the fire I'd survived wasn't a barrier—it was my bridge.

The rest of the session was a blur of tears, laughter, and raw honesty. The women in the room weren't just listening—they were *feeling* it with me. I could sense their hearts opening as mine did. When the coaching ended, I hugged her, shaky but lighter, as if I'd shed an invisible weight I hadn't known I carried.

As I walked back to my seat, still wiping tears from my cheeks, the first woman reached for my arm. "Because you shared your story," she said softly, "I can share mine." Another leaned in and whispered, "I thought I was the only one." More smiled, nodding, some with tears in their eyes. I sat down, hands trembling, realizing something sacred had just happened. My fear had turned into freedom—not just for me, but for them too.

That day, I learned that legacy doesn't begin when you've figured everything out. It begins the moment your truth gives someone else permission to speak theirs. My story didn't end on that stage—it multiplied. And I knew, deep in my bones, that the phoenix inside me wasn't just rising anymore. She was lighting the way for others to rise, too.

* * *

In the weeks that followed, I couldn't shake what had happened. I thought about those women often—the way their eyes filled with tears, the way they leaned in when I spoke. For the first time, I understood that my voice could carry healing, not just for me, but for others. It was humbling and powerful. I had spent so long believing that purpose belonged to people who had it all together. That day showed me the truth: The most powerful stories are the ones still being written.

When I began coaching, I carried that lesson with me. I promised myself I would lead with authenticity, not performance. My story wasn't a wound to hide—it was a bridge. Every client who sat across from me came carrying her own version of ashes: fear, exhaustion, loss, or self-doubt. My job wasn't to fix her. It was to help her find the ember still burning underneath.

A few months later, I received a message from a client who had been hesitant about her dreams—afraid to step fully into her potential. She had been dabbling in two business ideas, holding back because she didn't believe she could succeed. I had watched her wrestle with that doubt, seen the spark in her eyes even when her voice trembled. Then one morning, I opened my inbox to find her testimonial.

She wrote that through our coaching, she had finally found faith in herself again. That she had stopped questioning whether she was ready and simply decided to begin. She told me she had launched both businesses and was already booking multiple clients for each. I sat there reading her words, tears spilling down my face, my hand pressed to my heart. Her message wasn't just a thank-you—it was confirmation. Proof that the legacy I was building wasn't theoretical. It was alive.

In that moment, I realized legacy isn't measured in milestones—it's measured in impact. It's not about the number of followers or the size of the stage. It's about the lives touched, the chains broken, the courage awakened. Her breakthrough was a reflection of my own—a living testament that transformation multiplies when we share it. I wasn't just coaching women; I was helping them remember their fire.

Legacy, for me, has never been about achievement—it's about awakening. It's about showing generations older than me that it's never too late to heal or dream again. I've watched women who once believed their time had passed step into new seasons with boldness. I've watched younger women rise faster because they had examples of resilience before them. That's legacy—impact that flows in both directions, honoring where we've come from while shaping where we're going.

And beneath it all, legacy is spiritual. It's obedience to the nudge that says, *You were made for this.* It's the quiet agreement between the heart and the divine: to keep showing up, even when it's hard, even when the outcome is unknown. My legacy isn't written in accolades—it's written in lives changed, in women rising, in the echoes of truth that continue long after the conversation ends.

Every time I see another woman step into her purpose, I'm reminded that this was never just about me. It was about the flame being passed—story to story, heart to heart. My job was never to be the light for everyone—it was to spark the light within them. That, I've learned, is the truest form of legacy there is.

Teaching: Legacy as a Living Framework

Legacy isn't something you build at the end of your life. It's something you live every day. Most people think of legacy as what's left behind: the house, the career, the accolades, or the stories told after we're gone. But real legacy isn't carved in stone or written in titles. It's imprinted in the hearts you've touched, the lives you've influenced, and the light you've sparked in others. Legacy is a living thing. It grows with every choice you make in alignment with your purpose.

The phoenix has always reminded me that fire doesn't just destroy—it transforms. Legacy is that same flame carried forward. It's not about one grand moment of rebirth but about the continual rising that happens each time we choose purpose over fear, truth over comfort, and progress over perfection. Every time we show up authentically, we pass the flame to someone else. Legacy lives in that exchange.

1. Personal Legacy – The Inner Flame

Personal legacy begins with you—how you live, speak, and lead yourself. It's the alignment between who you are and how you show up. It's the quiet consistency between your words and your actions. Living this way doesn't mean perfection—it means truth. The more you live aligned with your values, the brighter your light shines.

From a neuroscience perspective, when you live aligned with your purpose, your brain's reward system activates. Dopamine and serotonin increase, reducing anxiety and strengthening confidence. Purpose literally rewires your brain for peace and fulfillment. That's why legacy starts within—it's not something you perform; it's something you embody.

2. Relational Legacy – The Shared Flame

Relational legacy is the imprint you leave on the people around you. It's how others experience your energy—how you listen, encourage, and lead with grace. You don't need a title to shape others. The way you raise your children, mentor a friend, or show compassion to a stranger becomes part of your living legacy. These small acts of rising ripple outward.

When you live authentically, you give others permission to do the same. Your courage becomes a mirror. Those around you begin to reflect the strength you've modeled. This is the fire spreading—quietly, powerfully, without force. Relational legacy is about creating environments where others can rise too.

3. Generational Legacy – The Eternal Flame

Generational legacy transcends time. It's what continues because you chose to live awake. It's not limited to biological families—it includes everyone influenced by your story and your work. Each decision you make in faith, each risk you take on purpose, each truth you speak aloud plants a seed in someone else's future. Generational legacy says, *Because I healed, they won't have to start from the same pain.*

The phoenix never keeps its flame to itself; it uses the fire to create new life. In the same way, your legacy isn't about what you keep—it's about what you give away. The energy you pour into others becomes your lasting impact. Legacy lives not in what burns down, but in what continues to rise after you.

4. The Faith Bridge – Living in Obedience to Purpose

Legacy doesn't grow from striving; it grows from surrender. When you stop chasing outcomes and start living in obedience to your calling, peace replaces pressure. This is where faith and purpose intersect. You don't have to see the entire path—just take the next right step. Obedience to purpose isn't passive; it's powerful. It's choosing to rise again and again, trusting that your light is enough for the moment you're in.

Living legacy this way transforms success into significance. It shifts the question from *What can I achieve?* to *Who am I becoming?* and *Whose life will be brighter because I was here?* The answers are written in every act of courage, compassion, and consistency.

The Legacy Mindset

Legacy requires more than inspiration—it asks for intention, discipline, and courage to keep the flame alive when life gets messy again. The truth is, even after you've risen, there will be seasons when the wind tries to dim your light. Legacy work isn't about maintaining perfection; it's about returning to purpose when everything else feels uncertain.

Stepping into legacy changed how I lead, create, and serve. It taught me that impact isn't built on constant motion—it's built on consistent alignment. I used to think success came from doing more. But I've learned that legacy grows deeper in the spaces where you pause, listen, and lead from clarity instead of chaos. Every leader must learn to protect the flame. That means honoring rest as much as action, and reflection as much as progress.

There are still moments when doubt whispers—*What if you run out of energy? What if you fail again?* But legacy isn't sustained by fear; it's fueled by faith. Every time I return to my why, every time I remind myself that my work is about impact, not image, the fire steadies. Legacy is leadership that endures because it's rooted in truth, not applause.

Purpose-driven leadership means living from conviction, not convenience. It's choosing to show up with integrity when no one's watching, and with grace when everyone is. It's understanding that sometimes the most powerful legacy moments aren't the ones caught on camera—they're the quiet ones: the late-night encouragement, the boundaries honored, the courage to say no to what doesn't serve your mission.

Legacy leadership also means evolving. The phoenix doesn't rise just once—it keeps rising, cycle after cycle, learning to trust the fire each time. As you grow, your legacy grows with you. Every season will call for new strength, new humility, new wisdom. True legacy isn't static; it's a living, breathing reflection of your continued transformation.

To sustain legacy, you must learn to hold both fire and gentleness. Burnout happens when we confuse drive with devotion. Drive pushes; devotion flows. Drive demands; devotion trusts. Legacy thrives in devotion—in that steady rhythm of showing up to serve, again and again, with a heart anchored in purpose.

So when the world feels heavy, return to your flame. When you wonder if your story still matters, look at the lives it's already touched. When you're tempted to hide again, remember: Someone is waiting for your light to remind them of their own. Legacy doesn't just rise—it radiates. And as long as you keep showing up with authenticity and courage, your flame will never go out.

Practices and Reflections

The Flame Check:
At the end of each week, ask yourself: Did I live aligned with my truth? Where did I dim my light, and where did I share it freely?

The Ripple List:
Write down three people you've impacted recently—through encouragement, service, or honesty. Let gratitude remind you how far your reach already extends.

The Rising Intention:
Each morning, set one small intention for how you'll embody legacy today. Maybe it's showing up with kindness, speaking the truth, or creating something that uplifts others. Legacy begins in those small, intentional moments.

* * *

Practices for Empowered Legacy

Lead Out Loud:
Share one piece of your story this week—in conversation, online, or within your community. Let your authenticity be the bridge someone else needs.

Light the Way:
Find one person you can mentor, encourage, or support. Offer your presence, not perfection. Legacy grows through shared fire.

Create a Ripple Ritual:

Each month, choose one small act of impact—volunteering, donating, or encouraging someone's dream. Track the ripples you create and celebrate them.

Legacy Audit:

Review your current commitments. Are they aligned with your purpose or draining your flame? Refine what no longer reflects who you're becoming.

Journal Prompts

1. How do I want others to feel after interacting with me?

    ____

    ____

2. What part of my story still feels too quiet and what truth wants to be spoken louder?

    ____

    ____

3. Who has been impacted by my growth, even indirectly?

    ____

    ____

4. What fears still keep me from sharing my gifts more boldly?

____

____

5. If I could define my living legacy in one sentence, what would it be?

____

____

CHAPTER ELEVEN

Becoming Her – The Embodied Rise

Lie: I'll feel ready when I've arrived.
Truth: Readiness comes from becoming her, now.

Declaration

I am no longer waiting to feel ready.

I am living as her, now.

I rise with confidence, move with intention, and lead with love.

The fire within me doesn't burn me—it fuels me.

I trust my timing, my intuition, and my truth.

I am both the spark and the steady flame.

I no longer chase who I want to be.

I embody her in every breath.

* * *

The morning of the Audacious Women's Summit felt different from any event I'd attended before. As sunlight spilled across my vanity, I looked at the outfit laid out before me—a dark pink blazer, black leather pants, and leopard print heels. Pieces I never would have worn eighteen months ago. Back then, I would have hidden behind muted tones and safe choices, anything that helped me blend into the background. But this time, I wasn't hiding. This time, I was showing up.

I slipped on the blazer, feeling its structure hug my shoulders like armor—but softer, truer. The color was bold, powerful, unapologetic. It wasn't just pink; it was a declaration. I added the final touch: a pair of large gold hoop earrings. When I bought them back in January

2025, I thought they were too much—too big, too loud, too *me*. Now they felt like a crown.

As I fastened them, I remembered the first time I met Lia, how her jewelry radiated confidence and purpose. Today, I wasn't just wearing her designs—I'd be taking photos with her, and she'd soon be designing jewelry for my RESET Live Retreat in 2026. It was more than a full-circle moment; it was a reminder that faith-filled alignment always leads us where we're meant to be.

When I arrived at the summit, the energy hit me like a wave—warm, alive, electric. The room buzzed with laughter and the hum of connection. Women hugged, cried, and cheered each other on. And as I stepped inside, heads turned. Not in the way that once made me shrink, but in a way that made me smile. I could feel it before anyone said a word: I had become her—the woman who walks into a room fully herself, no longer apologizing for taking up space.

Then I saw my friend, the host of the event. The sight of her on stage brought a rush of emotion I hadn't expected—pride in her accomplishment, gratitude for her belief in me, and awe at the way life weaves people together at just the right moments. The first time we met, I'd told her about my dream to leave my job and coach full-time. I remember the way she looked at me—eyes steady, unwavering. "You're going to do it," she said back then. "I already see it in you."

She had poured that belief into me when all I had was hope and a handful of what-ifs. She believed 1000% before I even believed 10%. Standing there now, watching her speak to a sold-out crowd of women, I realized just how much that belief had carried me. It had been one of the first sparks in the fire that became my rise.

Throughout the day, I was greeted by so many familiar faces—women who had witnessed every step of my transformation over the last eighteen months. They had seen me when I was still rebuilding, still questioning, still learning to trust my voice again. Now, they hugged me and whispered, "We can see the change in you." They told me they saw it in my eyes, in my words, in the way I carried myself. And I felt it, too. For the first time, I wasn't trying to prove I belonged. I *knew* I did.

When the award nominations were announced, I heard my name called: *Audacious Woman of the Year, 2025.* For a split second, I froze. Then the room erupted in applause, and I felt the tears sting my eyes. I wasn't overwhelmed—I was grounded. I was proud. The kind of pride that comes from walking through fire and knowing every ember had a purpose.

As I accepted the nomination, I thought about what "audacious" really means. It's not about being loud—it's about being brave. It's the courage to keep showing up when you're scared. It's choosing authenticity when it would be easier to hide. It's living in full color after years of gray.

The summit became more than an event. It was a mirror reflecting how much I'd grown. Every conversation that weekend felt divinely timed. I met women who instantly felt like sisters, collaborators, partners in purpose. Women who weren't competing—they were *connecting.* I knew, deep down, that many of them would be people I'd grow with for years to come. That realization filled me with a sense of peace I hadn't known before.

There was no striving, no proving—just belonging. I realized that being "Her" didn't mean reaching perfection. It meant embracing imperfection with confidence. It meant showing up with my whole heart and trusting that who I am today is enough for what's next.

At one point, I caught my reflection in a hallway mirror. For a moment, time slowed. I saw the same woman who once hid behind oversized clothes, unsure of her worth, trying to disappear. But now, standing in that pink blazer and those bold hoops, I didn't see a woman trying to be less—I saw one who finally gave herself permission to shine.

This was the embodiment. Not the loud kind that demands attention, but the quiet kind that radiates peace. The kind that says, "I'm not who I was, and I don't need to be. I've become her."

Later, as the event wound down, I stood near the stage beside Lia, both of us laughing as someone snapped photos. The weight of that moment hit me—how everything had come full circle. From buying her earrings in hesitation to wearing them with pride, from dreaming of coaching to building an empire rooted in purpose.

When I looked around the room, I saw hundreds of women shining in their own way—each one carrying her own flame, her own rise. The phoenix inside me didn't burn alone anymore. The fire wasn't something I carried *for* others—it burned *with* them.

This is what becoming her looks like: not an arrival, but an awakening. Not the end of transformation, but the continuation of it. I've learned that "Her" isn't a destination—it's a daily embodiment. Every morning that I choose gratitude, courage, and truth, I become her again. Every time I pour into another woman, I expand her reach.

As I left the summit, I walked out into the evening air feeling both powerful and peaceful. The lights from the building shimmered against the dark sky, and I couldn't help but smile. The woman who once questioned her worth had become the woman who no longer needed permission.

I am her—audacious, aligned, and alive. And the most beautiful part? I know this isn't the end. It's only the next rise.

Teaching: Living as Her – The Power of Embodiment

Becoming her isn't about becoming someone new. It's about remembering who you've always been beneath the fear, the conditioning, and the noise. It's not an act of striving—it's an act of returning.

For most of my life, I thought transformation was a finish line. I believed there would be a day when I finally arrived—where all the healing, growth, and hard work would settle into a neat, permanent version of me. But what I've learned is that embodiment doesn't come from the arrival—it comes from the repetition. From showing up for yourself again and again until "becoming her" stops being a decision and starts being your default.

The science behind it is powerful. Every time you choose a thought, a routine, or a response that aligns with the woman you want to be, you're literally rewiring your brain. Neuroplasticity allows your mind to build new patterns of confidence, calm, and courage. What used to trigger fear or doubt begins to feel familiar and safe because you've taught your nervous system what truth feels like. This is embodiment on a physiological level—when your body, mind, and spirit all agree on who you are.

It's why routines matter. The morning walk. The journaling. The moments of stillness. The way you speak to yourself before you speak to anyone else. Each small act is an anchor—a signal to your brain and body that you are no longer surviving; you're living with intention.

But embodiment isn't rigid. It's not about locking yourself into a fixed identity. It's about *flowing* with purpose. There will still be days when you forget, when you slip back into old patterns or doubt yourself.

The difference now is that you know how to find your way home. "Her" isn't a costume you put on. It's the truth you return to.

From a soulful perspective, embodiment is the divine partnership between surrender and action. It's saying, "I trust the timing, but I also trust myself." It's releasing the idea that you need permission or perfection before moving forward. The woman you're becoming doesn't wait until she's fearless. She acts in faith, even when fear still whispers.

One of the most important lessons I've learned about embodiment is that confidence doesn't arrive first—it follows consistency. Every time you choose to align your actions with your truth, you strengthen your self-trust. You stop performing and start *living*. You stop chasing approval and start *radiating peace*.

Becoming her is not about being louder or bolder for the sake of it. It's about being rooted—so grounded in your authenticity that you no longer need to prove it. It's that quiet confidence that fills a room before you even speak. It's the energy that comes from wholeness, not hustle.

The phoenix inside you doesn't rise once—it learns to live in the flame. Embodiment is that ongoing rise. It's the knowing that you can walk through the fire without losing yourself, because now, the fire lives within you. You've become the light you were chasing.

When I look at the woman I've become, I see both strength and softness. I still feel fear, but it no longer dictates my direction. I've learned that being her isn't about having all the answers—it's about trusting that I'm capable of finding them. It's about grace in the growth, resilience in the becoming, and gratitude in the now.

Living as her means showing up for your life every single day like it's already yours. It means loving yourself enough to maintain the habits, the boundaries, and the beliefs that built your rise. It's the balance between rest and ambition, between doing and being.

You don't become her by waiting for the right time. You become her every time you choose courage over comfort, truth over illusion, alignment over approval. Every time you act from faith instead of fear, you're embodying her.

This is the heart of embodiment: It's not what you achieve—it's who you *allow* yourself to be.

Practices and Reflections

Practices for Living as Her

The Mirror Practice – See Her, Speak to Her, Be Her

Each morning, before the noise of the day begins, meet yourself in the mirror. Not the version that critiques or corrects, but the woman who's still standing. Look into your eyes until you see her: the woman you've fought to become. Speak to her. Remind her that she's strong, worthy, radiant, and ready. Some mornings, your reflection will look tired or unsure but that's okay. "Her" doesn't need perfection; she needs presence. I still do this every morning before an event or podcast taping, not to hype myself up, but to anchor myself in truth. The more often you practice seeing her, the easier it becomes to live as her.

The Energy Check – Embody the Frequency of Who You Are Becoming

Throughout the day, pause and ask: *How does she feel?* When "Her" is in alignment, you'll notice it—your breath slows, your body relaxes, your mind quiets. When you feel rushed, anxious, or disconnected, gently return to that frequency. Sometimes, I realign by adjusting my posture, taking three slow breaths, or listening to music that grounds me before I speak or coach. You don't have to force confidence; you just need to reconnect to the energy of peace that already exists within you.

The Alignment Audit – Live in Agreement with Your Values

Once a month, reflect on where your energy is going. Look at your commitments, relationships, and goals. Do they align with the woman you're becoming? "Her" knows when to release what no longer fits. I've learned that staying in alignment often requires saying 'no' to good things so I can say 'yes' to the right ones. Audit your calendar, your conversations, and even your self-talk. If it doesn't feed your flame, it's time to let it go.

The Sacred Routine – Protect What Grounds You

Embodiment isn't glamorous—it's sacred consistency. My sacred routines are simple but powerful: journaling in the morning light, sipping tea in stillness, and choosing my outfit with intention. I used to dress to hide; now I dress to express. Whether it's a pink blazer, a pair of bold earrings, or comfortable clothes that make you feel strong, let your external reflection reflect your internal. Build routines that nurture your health, your energy, and your creativity. "Her" thrives in rhythm, not chaos.

The Phoenix Practice – Rise, Rest, Repeat

When life feels heavy again—and it will—don't question the fire. Let it refine you, not define you. I've learned that becoming her isn't about never falling; it's about knowing how to rise with grace. When burnout whispers, pause. When doubt returns, breathe. The phoenix never fears the ashes; she trusts the rise. The cycle of rising, resting, and renewing is what sustains your embodiment over time.

Reflection Questions:

Take these slowly. This chapter is about discernment, not urgency.

- What part of myself feels more awake or honest after this chapter?
- Where am I still holding onto an old identity because it feels familiar, even though it no longer fits?
- What have I been confusing with strength that is actually self-protection?
- When I imagine living aligned with what I now know to be true, what feels exciting and what feels threatening?
- What patterns am I being invited to outgrow, not shame, or fix, but gently release?
- Where in my life am I being asked to respond differently than I have before?
- What does self-trust look like for me right now, in real daily choices, not in theory?
- What am I learning about my capacity to change without burning everything down?
- How has my understanding of healing, growth, or faith shifted since earlier chapters?
- If I stopped waiting to feel "ready," what would be my next right step?

Discernment Reflection: Listening for What Matters

Answer honestly, even if the answers surprise you.

- What feels non-negotiable for my well-being moving forward?
- What am I tolerating that is quietly costing me peace or clarity?

- What support, structure, or boundary do I need more of right now?

Integration Prompt

Finish this sentence without overthinking it:

"This chapter is asking me to choose _________________ instead of _________________."

Let that answer guide how you move into the next chapter, not with pressure, but with intention.

Journal Prompts

1. When do I feel most connected to the woman I'm becoming?

____

____

2. What habits, beliefs, or relationships no longer align with "Her"?

____

____

3. How do I speak to myself when no one's listening—and how can I make that voice more compassionate?

____

____

5. What does "living in full expression" look like for me right now?

____

____

6. How can I protect my peace while still expanding my purpose?

____

____

7. Where do I still hide, and what would happen if I stopped?

____

____

8. How can I honor the version of me who fought to get here, while still giving myself permission to evolve?

____

____

Choose Truth, Healing, and Purpose

If you're reading this, take a deep breath. Let it settle into your chest—the truth that you've already begun.

You didn't need to finish this book to start your transformation. You started the moment you said, *I want more.*

You've walked through the pages of pain and purpose, through stories that may have mirrored your own. You've seen how healing is not a straight line—it's a spiral that keeps leading you back to the truth of who you are. You've learned that you are not behind; you are becoming.

The lies that once held you small don't get the final word. You do. Because the rise isn't about waiting for the perfect moment—it's about choosing truth, again and again. It's the quiet decision to keep showing up for your life, even when it feels messy or uncertain. Healing isn't about going back to who you were—it's about honoring who you're becoming.

You've seen by now that your purpose doesn't demand perfection. It asks for presence.
You've learned that your worth isn't tied to your productivity or your past—it's anchored in your existence.
You've witnessed that courage doesn't roar; sometimes it whispers, *I'll try again tomorrow.*

So this is my invitation to you:
Keep rising.
Keep choosing truth over noise, healing over hustle, and peace over proving.

Let your faith be stronger than your fear.
Let your story be the spark that lights the way for others.

And when you forget who you are—which you will, sometimes—come back here. Read these words again. Remember that every chapter you've lived, even the hardest ones, has been preparing you for this moment.

You are not who you were when you started these pages. You have already become more.

You are the phoenix—rising, radiant, unshaken.
You don't have to earn the next chapter. You just have to live it.

Final Affirmation

My life is mine to design.
I am ready to rise.
I am ready to live.
I am ready to become.

The lie may have been loud.
But your truth?
It was always louder.

About the Author

Monica Connolly is a transformational speaker, coach, and author known as The Transformation Catalyst Coach. After surviving profound loss, navigating chronic illness, and overcoming binge eating disorder, Monica rebuilt her life from the inside out—losing 150 pounds, reclaiming her health, and rising into her purpose. Today she helps women silence the lies that keep them small and step into the truth of who they were created to be.

Through her coaching programs, podcast Unshakeable Belief, and speaking engagements, Monica empowers audiences around the world to reset their health, rewire their mindset, and rise into purpose with unshakable faith. Her work has been featured in best-selling anthologies, women's leadership platforms, and faith-driven communities, where her voice blends grit and grace, truth and hope.

She is the Founder & CEO of Monica Connolly Coaching and lives out her mission daily: to help women heal from the inside out and live boldly, on purpose.

Continue the Journey

If you've made it to this page, something in you is already listening differently.

Awareness is powerful.
But transformation happens when awareness is practiced, supported, and lived.

That's why I host **free monthly masterclasses and virtual events** designed to help you move from noise to clarity, from survival to steadiness, and from self-doubt to embodied confidence.

These sessions are a space to:

- Slow down and reconnect with yourself
- Learn nervous-system-aware tools you can actually use
- Deepen the work you've begun in this book
- Be reminded that you are not alone in this process

Join Me Live

To see what's coming up next and register for a **free masterclass**, scan the QR code below.

This page is always updated with the most current event, so you can return anytime and join us when the timing feels right.

A Final Reminder

You don't need to rush your healing.
You don't need to have it all figured out.
You don't need to become someone new.

You only need to keep choosing truth over noise.

The lie may be loud.
But your truth is steady.

And when you're ready to take the next step, I'll be there to meet you.

— Monica Connolly
Author of *The Lie Is Loud*
Transformation Catalyst Coach